# WHY LEADERS

# FAIL

## SCIENCE REVEALS THE SURE SIGNS OF FAILURE AND PREPARES YOU FOR SUCCESS

David Sullivan, Ph.D

Don Double, M.A.

Jonathan Magid

ISBN: 1-4392-5244-0
ISBN-13: 9781439252444

# FOREWORD

Dave Sullivan, a long-time friend, along with co-authors Don Double and Jonathan Magid, all of whose solid records of leadership study, consulting and coaching I deeply respect, asked me if I would try my hand at designing cover art and writing the *Foreword* for their book on leadership. I gave them an immediate "No" and "Yes." I declined the artsy part, based upon both the years since I have exercised my artistic "talents" and a clear understanding of their limits; and, I accepted the *Foreword*-writing part as a simple assignment that I could pump out with little effort.

My quick decision yielded a "right" and a "wrong." My "good call:" you really don't want me drawing anything that would linger in public view. My "not so good call:" I have been staring at the computer screen for several days, trying to figure out exactly what to say about their approach to this very big subject, and about this book. Like everyone else on this planet (all of whom seem to have written at least one book on leadership), I have my own belief system on what makes for good leadership and what makes good leaders. And since it is *my* belief system, I am quite attached to it.

But alas, it appears this self-satisfaction may not be warranted. So let me get this out of the way: what we think makes for great leadership and leaders, the "truths" we have preached for years, often sound better than they work. If you or I have actually been on target with part or all of our beliefs about leadership, that probably occurred at the random intersection of time, observation and luck.

Why? Because our beliefs are not likely supported by rigorous study or significant statistical evidence. We have observed or read about men and women who are alleged to have exercised excellent leadership, and we thus assume their unique style, techniques and characteristics are keys to leadership. But wait: we know from experience that if we line up 100 so-called top leaders, we would find a *wide range* of leadership styles. So do we need all of these elements to lead? If not, which are the keys to leadership? Or does it matter – can we lead well with any two, three or four of these techniques?

On top of all of this wondering, serious scholars now question the validity of books on business success and leadership, including some of the best known and most respected. Their concern is based on what they see as the lack of rigor behind these publications. Critics claim these writings are based heavily on the heroes' own stated principles, stories shared by loyal followers, and limited time periods; and, we too easily assume that success derived from the "leader's" traits (when, in fact, success may have made the traits look like "leadership"). I would add that an ongoing hunger for "silver bullets" – easy explanations and easy solutions – has fueled this love affair.

In fact, the point of the authors study and this book is that *there are a few leadership traits which have provable positive impact over time, and a few that erode results.* While we are all unique, with different personalities and (yes) "styles," the key elements present in leadership are few and provable, i.e., there is statistically significant evidence that a few elements we associate with leadership *do* influence positive results, and a few also lead to poor (documented) results.

None of this requires me to give up my respect for Abraham Lincoln, Winston Churchill, Warren Bennis or Jack Welch. They and countless others have remarkable results associated with their time "at the top." However, I believe if you look carefully at their choices, decisions and actions, you will find that the elements described in this book pop up with great frequency in their body of work. And it is for this – their instinct for and/or the understanding of what really matters in their role as leader – that the highly regarded deserve recognition and praise.

For those of you who aspire to lead, I suggest you read the book. Sullivan, Double and Magid can explain the key principles – **The Magic Triangle** and **The Tragic Triangle** – as well as the research underpinning their recommendations, far better than can I. Meanwhile, I am going to take these principles out into the world and try them on, while quietly hanging on to one of my "pet beliefs" – that if I turn around, and no one is following me, I'm probably not leading. Enjoy!

*Larry Cassidy*
Chair, Vistage International

Larry Cassidy has been a Chair with Vistage International (formerly TEC International) for over 22 years. He has facilitated over 1000 executive advisory group meetings, and participated in almost 10,000 face-to-face discussions with chief executives about all aspects of their businesses. He has received numerous awards including Chair Excellence (9 years), Star, designation as Master Chair, and the Don Cope Award, the highest recognition given to active Chairs. The former Marine Corps officer has worked for a number of public companies (General Mills, Quaker Oats, and PepsiCo) as well as serving as General Manager and CEO of Los Angeles based companies. Larry is a leader's leader.

# CONTENTS

## THE LEADERSHIP SUCCESS INDICATOR

# STOP!
## Before you turn the page, read this important note.

The Leadership Success Indicator (LSI) is a scientifically-valid, rigorously-tested self-assessment instrument that will help you get the most out of reading this book. It will take you no more than 10 minutes to complete. As a purchaser of the book you are welcome to use the link below to access the LSI and complete it. Once we receive your completed assessment, we will score it and return the results to you electronically within 48 hours.

Throughout the book you will use the results of your Leadership Success Indicator assessment to craft a customized, personal, rigorous leadership development plan that, if you follow its steps thoughtfully and thoroughly, will speed your journey toward becoming an Exemplary Leader.

Please take 10 minutes right now to take the assessment.

# http://www.whyleadersfail.com/ bookbuyers/freelsi.html

# INTRODUCTION

## SCIENCE EXPLAINS WHY LEADERS FAIL... AND PREPARES YOU FOR SUCCESS

Let's acknowledge something right away: there are hundreds of books about leadership. We wrote this book because we've studied leaders in great detail for more than a decade, and we've noticed that as great as so many leadership books are, almost all of them suffer from one or more of these few common problems:

- They are autobiographical, and thus based on one celebrity executive's experience and opinion
- They are historical reviews, and thus based on one person's research and point of view about great leaders from the past, or
- They are subjective theories of leadership based on one expert's ideas and experiences with leaders great and small.

Now, to be fair we believe that celebrity executives usually got that way because they're great at something. In fact, they're probably great at a lot of things. Nearly everyone who reads one of these books – think Jack, Straight from the Gut by Jack Welch, or Leadership by Rudy Giuliani – has learned something from them. Chances are, though, that Jack Welch isn't running your business, and though he's not short of clients, it's not likely that Rudy Giuliani is consulting with you.

We also believe that reading about history's great leaders is a worthwhile and even important use of time. Who hasn't wanted to emulate history's most luminous figures, particularly when they have names like Peter the Great instead of Ivan the Terrible? We believe strongly that the lessons in A Team of Rivals, Doris Kearns Goodwin's biographical study of Abraham Lincoln and his contentious cabinet, are powerful, essential calls to action for today's leaders. Let's be frank: we're people with a bias for science and the observance of facts, and we say with confidence that you are not Abraham Lincoln and neither is that guy sleeping next to you in 22E on your flight to LaGuardia.

Reading people's opinions about what made them successful provides great food for thought and conversation. The things you learn might even improve your leadership performance. Then again, they might not – after all, they're the experiences and opinions of *someone else* who worked under different circumstances, and who's now writing through his or her own filters, interpretations, and biases. You can take action on what you learn from these books, but it's not possible to predict how that action will impact your performance, or even whether or not it's something worth working on. What's missing in these books is the edge that science brings – predictable improvement and a reliable guide of what skills or behaviors to improve.

In this book, we bring you that scientific edge.

The scientific study of leadership is a tricky business. Research so often looks at so many different behaviors, all of which influence each other, that the results are a complicated mess. Everything seems important, and researchers don't want to leave out something important! The typical result from books based on studies of leaders has often been a weighty model of 16, 21, or even more behaviors or competencies that leaders "must master" in order to be effective. Because they are so complex, these models don't allow much room for the nuances of a particular organization's culture. Often, leaders who read these books are faced with conflicts and conundrums, particularly when it comes to identifying the few areas where making some improvements will really yield progress.

When we set out to write this book, we wanted to deliver not just good science, but science that our readers could put to good use. This book is based on years of statistical analysis, executive coaching with thousands of individual leaders, and work with hundreds of groups in organizations worldwide. Our research shows convincingly that the path to exemplary leadership is straightforward (okay, hold it: notice we said "straightforward," not "easy." No one is promising you a cakewalk here. Straightforwardness and degree of difficulty are not correlated!). The best leaders in the world consistently do a few things better than others. The worst leaders in the world also consistently do a few things, but they do them worse than others. By taking the self-assessment before you read the book (if you haven't, please stop reading and take the assessment at http://www.whyleadersfail.com/bookbuyers/freelsi.html), and then, using your self-assessment results to create your own leadership development plan, you can and will improve your leadership performance.

It's well known that leadership matters. As individuals, great leaders stand out in our minds and in our experience because they inspire our best work and because they help us to reach our fullest potential. In groups, great leaders are memorable for bringing teams together and getting everyone moving in the same direction, seeming almost magically to help individuals overcome obstacles in the service of the team's goals. In large organizations great leaders are often known as effective visionaries, people who inspire a shared sense of a vital future and who show and then clear the path to get there, building teams of teams along the way. Leadership performance is highly correlated with organizational performance in virtually every dimension, no matter how it is studied, measured, or reported.

We'd sometimes like to think that when we read one of the many books on leadership, we'll find the keys to the leadership kingdom, and in a flash, we'll be transformed into great leaders – and then heralded as such by our many friends and minions, marched into the corner office (now our own, of course), given a seven-figure raise and the stewardship of a giant division or the whole company, and turned loose to spread our logic and our wisdom down and outward through our organizations. We'd like to think that this is possible, just as we'd like to think that being a center fielder like Willie Mays is possible too. Who wouldn't like to be the Say Hey Kid, or Richard Branson, or Jack Welch?

This book promises that precious little is truly out of reach. You might never play center field for a big-league ball club, and you might never become the CEO of a Fortune 100 company, but you CAN be an exemplary leader. You can be the kind of person who others look back on and say, "The best boss I ever worked for was Cathy T. Cathy knew exactly where our group was going, she had my complete confidence, and she got my best work almost all the time, and the best from other people too. She brought us together in a united purpose, and she gave us enough rope, but never pushed us off the cliff, either."

This book also promises that mastering leadership is hard work, and that it requires courage, commitment, and candor. If you're in it for yourself, or if your job demands that you develop the people around you into leaders – and by the way, that's exactly what your job demands of you if you intend to lead more than just a few people at any time – then this book offers you the opportunity to unlock the mysteries of leadership and apply a few straightforward tools and structures that, if you use them and if you practice, will make you a better leader, and will help you develop better leaders around you.

We've built this book and the thinking that underlies it on extensive research and work with more than 10,000 leaders, good and bad, around the world, conducted over the past 15 years. This work involved collecting and analyzing 360-degree feedback and providing executive coaching in 1-on-1 sessions. These are people at multiple levels of leadership ranging from supervisory, first-time managers all the way to the top-level executives you read about in *Fortune, Forbes,* and, *Fast Company.*

You can read the full details of our study in the appendix. Here's the overview:

During the course of our study, we identified the top-rated 10% of participants as "Exemplary Leaders" and the bottom-rated 10% as "Failed Leaders." With these groups identified, we set out to discover what made them the best or the worst of the lot. We also compared their ratings to their business results as rated by their colleagues, and found further confirmation that leadership behavior does indeed directly influence business performance.

We examined these leaders against 19 behavioral competencies, or groups of behaviors. The full definition for each of these competencies is found in the appendix. The competencies themselves are as follows:

- ➢ **Aligns Strategy and Planning**
- ➢ **Analyzes Issues**
- ➢ **Attracts and develops talent**
- ➢ **Builds Relationships**
- ➢ **Champions continuous improvement**
- ➢ **Communicates Effectively**
- ➢ **Communicates the Vision**
- ➢ **Demonstrates Adaptability and Flexibility**
- ➢ **Demonstrates Self Development**
- ➢ **Drives for Results**
- ➢ **Empowers**
- ➢ **Fosters Teamwork**
- ➢ **Innovates**
- ➢ **Inspires Confidence**
- ➢ **Leads Courageously**
- ➢ **Motivates**
- ➢ **Negotiates and Influences**
- ➢ **Thinks Strategically**
- ➢ **Values Diversity**

Interestingly, while the Exemplary group outscored the Failed group by a statistically significant margin in every competency, we found six competencies in total that most clearly drove success or failure for each of these two groups. The Exemplary Leaders were rated highest in three competencies consistently throughout the study. The Failed Leaders failed most of all, or put another way were rated lowest, in a separate set of three competencies. We came to call these the "Magic Triangle" and "Tragic Triangle" respectively. As our work progressed through the study of how these competencies are correlated, we've seen that they work together. These two sets of three competencies form a "Golden Triangle" of Leadership Excellence.

## The Magic Triangle: Where the Exemplary Leaders rate highest
- *Inspires Confidence*
- *Builds Relationships*
- *Drives for Results*

7

**The Tragic Triangle: Where the Failed Leaders rate lowest**
- *Communicates the Vision*
- *Fosters Teamwork*
- *Empowers*

This concept forms the core of the book: being effective at the "Tragic Triangle" competencies of *Communicates the Vision, Fosters Teamwork,* and *Empowers* creates the foundation of Leadership Effectiveness. On that foundation, one can then build excellence in the "Magic Triangle" competencies of *Inspires Confidence, Builds Relationships,* and *Drives for Results.* If you do not establish at least a baseline level of effectiveness at the "Tragic Triangle" competencies, it is very unlikely – perhaps even impossible – for you to become an Exemplary Leader. In fact, you will most likely become a Failed Leader. The "Tragic Triangle" competencies are to leadership as blocking and tackling are to football, or passing and dribbling to basketball: they are core fundamentals. You must spend time and effort to ensure that you do these basic things well before you can realize your fullest potential.

Of course, the reason why achieving leadership greatness is even harder than achieving your best in sport is because your leadership exists entirely in the experience of those around you, and fully understanding that experience, let alone influencing it, requires powerful skill in the subtle arts of interpersonal relationships. Because "Builds Relationships" is one of the three "Magic Triangle" competencies, rest assured we'll spend significant time on it through the book.

With the study and analysis complete, we then went looking for examples of people who have successfully changed their leadership behavior and realized increased business success as a result. We have been fortunate to study many people over extended periods of time and to see the real-life results of their attempts to change their own leadership behavior. This book follows their successes and failures as well.

We've relied on 360-degree feedback in no small part because research clearly shows that the best predictor of leadership success is the ratings of one's peers and direct reports (Hogan et al. 1994). For the uninitiated, 360-degree feedback processes elicit confidential ratings on all those traits, behaviors and business practices that the company and its expert consultants deem essential to business success. The traits, behaviors, and business practices are generally organized into natural groupings called "competencies."

360-degree feedback instruments always ask the individual participant to rate him or herself on the same instrument. One of the most interesting aspects of any 360 report, and of course of any detailed study of this kind of feedback, is the deviance between self- and other raters' ratings. It is remarkable to see the degree to which our self-perceptions quite frequently differ from the perceptions of those around us. This is particularly important for the study of leadership, given that a leader's effectiveness depends almost entirely on the willing action of those he or she leads. As it turns out, the people we seem to know least well are ourselves.

During our study we discovered something vastly more important than the simple fact that there is wide variance between others' perceptions and our own. Indeed, among the array of interesting and useful findings about self- versus other-ratings, we found that the Exemplary Leaders and Failed Leaders had very specific, statistically significant patterns, not only of variance in ratings, but also in specific patterns of self-perceptions.

The fact that Exemplary and Failed leaders answered questions about themselves differently than the members of their opposite group led us to develop a self-rating instrument that accurately predicts an individual's potential for leadership success. That's the assessment that you saw at the very beginning of the book. Throughout the book, you will use your results from that instrument to begin designing your own, custom leadership development plan. If you haven't done so already, please complete the self-assessment before you read further to get the most value from this book. We've designed it to be both a useful tool for developing enhanced self-awareness, and importantly also to support the hiring, selection, and development of leaders around you.

# CHAPTER I

## THE TRAGIC TRIANGLE OF LEADERSHIP FAILURE

"…leadership only occurs in the experience of those being led"

*Rita was a key Human Resources executive for a large technology company that had enjoyed explosive growth. As the company sought to consolidate its gains through more mature processes, Rita wanted to strengthen the HR organization with a more centralized structure as well as systems, processes, and tools that could be shared by all the company's many divisions. Rita sensed that the heads of the divisions, who essentially ran their own businesses and who had built their own HR teams over the years, weren't ready for that big a change all at once, so she put her direct reports to work building some centralized processes and created a council of major divisional representatives to help her guide the creation of the new approach.*

*While Rita's central HR team worked toward their goals as she assigned them, Rita often took direction from the committee she had put together, and frequently changed her own team's assignments to suit what she believed the committee wanted. Responding to the rising frustration on her team, Rita often changed her own team's structure, reporting relationships, priorities, and assignments, letting rivalries build and fester among her team. Ultimately, there would be no centralization, as a larger company bought Rita's firm.*

*When the new firm's executive assessment team came in to conduct their reviews, they were shocked to learn how Rita's team and colleagues viewed her. Her direct reports were fearful or hostile toward her; her colleagues felt she was ineffective and her entire function should have been sacked. The executive assessment team quickly came to a stark conclusion: Rita was a failed leader.*

Here's an easy cocktail-party challenge: ask three people to tell you a story about a bad boss they've had, and see how long it takes your small group to turn into the largest, loudest conversation ring at the party. We're guessing it won't take very long at all. Why's that? Because as you know, everyone has had the "bad-boss experience." Beyond the natural desire to one-up each other with horror stories of workplace drama writ large, these stories evoke a great deal of empathy – or sometimes schadenfreude, or heck, even both – and we think that's tragic.

Even more tragic is the damage that failed leaders do. Year in and year out, the news is jammed with stories of CEOs who have led their companies down the tubes. Failed leaders destroy value for everyone: shareholders are left poorer, customers are left in the lurch, and employees, most of all, suffer from everything from simple disengagement (the costs of which are increasingly evident in research that's turning up all over) to outright loss of income thanks to layoffs caused by blundering management. Failed leaders are a cancer on the body of business.

As we have written, we didn't set out to study leadership failure. We set out wanting to know what made the best leaders exactly that: the best. Our hypothesis was that the best leaders would share some significant traits and behaviors in common. They do. We also discovered, though, that leadership failure has its roots in common traits and behaviors too. We didn't expect to see such commonality among failed leaders, but we did see it, and we have seen it repeated in all of our work with executives and managers since. Why do leaders fail? It's simple: true, they are "worse" in nearly all ways than most others. But more importantly, there are specific behavioral areas that appear to drive leaders directly down the road to ruin.

The failed leaders in our study rated lower than the rest of the cohort in the study in every competency. In all cases, these differences were statistically significant. That means that the differences were bigger than could be ascribed to chance. There were three competencies, however, where the failed leader group rated so much lower, and so consistently lower, than all others in the study, that it was clear that this was a significant part of the basis for their failure.

The failed leaders were rated lowest in these three competencies:
- **Communicates the Vision**
- **Fosters Teamwork**
- **Empowers**

We'll examine each of these competencies in some detail in a few moments, but right now we invite you just to think about those three areas of behavior, and how they relate to leadership. We're confident that you're not altogether surprised that people who fail to communicate a vision, who fail to engender cooperation between people and groups, and who fail to give others the power and authority to do their jobs effectively just aren't very good people to follow. It's not a shocker.

Our research shows these three areas are so essential to leadership success that to fail in one or more of these areas virtually guarantees that you cannot succeed as a leader. Think of it this way: if you want to be successful in any given discipline, first, you must become competent. Very few people might ever become as great a cellist as Yo Yo Ma, but if you have aspirations even to join a community string quartet, first you must learn how to play the instrument. It's no different with leadership – if you fail at the basics you cannot possibly succeed, and these three competencies are the basics.

Let's also take a moment here to reflect again on the fact that leadership only occurs in the experience of those being led. We'll take the risk of you getting tired of reading that because we believe it is so critically important to understand. Your behavior obviously matters – the things you say, do, and indicate with non-verbal cues. The reason why your behavior matters, though, is that the people around you see, hear, and otherwise experience that behavior. Naturally, their own beliefs, experiences, and filters have the greatest influence on how they interpret the messages you send. In the chapter about "changing how you change," we'll have more to say about understanding others' experience of you and plotting a successful course of behavior change. For now, however, we ask that you keep in mind that it is always and only the experience of those around a leader that makes the leader successful.

Recall that our failed leader group scored lower across the board than their counterparts in the study. More importantly, though, they scored particularly low in the three competencies we mentioned above – Communicates the Vision, Fosters Teamwork, and Empowers.

Within each competency group are sets of individual behaviors or traits that contribute to the overall score in that group. We list those below.

### Communicates the Vision:
- Conveys a sense of mission that inspires and motivates others
- Expresses confidence in future actions and direction of the organization
- Freely and regularly shares strategic business information throughout the organization

### Fosters Teamwork:
- Involves others in planning and decision-making
- Builds cooperative teams in which group members feel valued and empowered and have shared goals
- Attracts and recruits the right people for the right assignments
- Promotes collaboration between functional areas.

### Empowers:
- Delegates authority and responsibility appropriately
- Supports others in carrying out their responsibilities

### Communicates the Vision:
It's not difficult to understand how failing to communicate a vision would make it very difficult to succeed as a leader. Some time ago we worked with Stan, an executive overseeing technical support functions for a telecommunications company. He had been successful as a small-market executive and had been assigned to a larger market that was struggling. Stan was seen at the time as someone who could turn it around. A year into the role, Stan hadn't succeeded and didn't understand why. In his smaller market, Stan knew everyone and had no difficulty picking up the phone to reach out to clients, suppliers, team-

mates, and other members of the community. Not so in this middle-market role, where his team seemed to be constantly at one another's throats and where rivalries between middle-markets and core, large market functions festered openly.

When we came in to assess the situation we saw early on that Stan had failed to create a vision for change. Members of his team reported that while he talked about the turnaround in the market, he did so in vague, indefinite terms. They knew that Stan was there to "fix what was wrong" with the division, but they didn't know what that looked like in Stan's mind. Without an end-point in mind, they didn't know what was important and what wasn't. No vision of success means that there is no real path to follow, and as the old saying goes, "if you don't know where you're going, you're probably going to end up somewhere else."

We're convinced that people enjoy sports so much in part because the goals are exceptionally clear. The vision for a football team, for example, is precise, specific, and definitive: win the Super Bowl. The path to that point is similarly clear: win games. Score more points than your opponent. The means to score points is equally transparent. Make more touchdowns, field goals, and safeties than your opponent, and you win.

As we know in the business world things are somewhat different. Sure, there's a scoreboard: the quarterly earnings report in public companies is one way to keep score, but the ways to score points become awfully complicated, awfully fast. A key task for the leader who wants to avoid failure is to cut through that complexity, to simplify, clarify, and spell out what the "Super Bowl victory" looks like in the context of the workplace. That's the vision.

With the end-state vision in place, it's easier obviously to spell out what constitutes a game won, a touchdown or a field goal, or other important measure in the context of that vision. It's also a lot easier to handle the inevitable changes that come along in a dynamic organization. Even if the vision has to change, provided you've done a good job in the experience of those around you at communicating the initial

15

vision, you're likely to be able to communicate the changes, the reasons behind them, and their impact as you and your team move forward.

Think back to Stan and his struggles for a moment. When he was brought in to turn the market around, he inherited a team of people who knew their market wasn't making sufficient progress. Stan missed the opportunity to spell out clearly what it would look like to be a high-performing market. Instead, he relied his own internal sense that he had gotten the job done elsewhere, so clearly he could do it here.

Unquestionably, there were projects and efforts related to those projects. Without a compelling vision of what the group would look like when the turnaround was complete, however, the people working for Stan didn't understand how his direction fit into a broader context. Worse, Stan's indefinite but oft-repeated calls for "change" and "turn-around" left people feeling threatened and undermined. Relationships failed as people acted on their fears and doubts.

Ultimately Stan was removed from the position and reassigned to a smaller market in a more junior role. It was the best decision for the company, but Stan's career suffered. The sad part is that it didn't have to suffer if Stan had understood the reasons why leaders fail.

Communicating the Vision sounds simple, and in fact it doesn't need to be difficult. Key elements must be in place for a vision to develop and then be communicated successfully. First, remember the three components in the "Communicates the Vision" competency:

- Conveys a sense of mission that inspires and motivates others
- Expresses confidence in future actions and direction of the organization
- Freely and regularly shares strategic business information throughout the organization

*Conveys a sense of mission that inspires and motivates others:*
In our example, it's easy to see that Stan failed to create a sense of mission. It's equally easy to see that he probably thought that he had created one – certainly, he spoke with passion and urgency about

the need to turn the division around. Two keys are essential here: the sense of mission must reference accomplishments, outcomes, or end-states, and the sense of mission must be understood and accepted broadly by the team in question.

If this sounds like establishing "clarity" to you, that's good. It's exactly what we're all looking for in a vision. Again, back to sports: does a vision get any clearer than "let's win the Super Bowl?" It does not. Successful leaders in organizations define what "winning the Super Bowl" means in the context of their organization, and then find ways to reinforce and support that vision and to track progress clearly toward it.

To excel at creating a sense of mission that inspires and motivates others, the first thing strong leaders do is find out what success looks like to them. Imagine how different Stan's experience would have been if he had started out in his new role by meeting with his direct reports and asking them individually what the division would look like if it successfully turned itself around?

If he had started there, Stan could have "compared notes" with his direct reports, identifying the areas where their notions of success dovetailed with his own, and matched up with larger, corporate goals. He could also have identified and resolved potential conflicts and identified likely challenges that might come between the team and its goals. This would have given everyone the opportunity to participate in forming, understanding, and accepting the vision for the group, and it would have created the clarity that was otherwise missing. Stan could have defined, with the participation and support of others, the "Super Bowl" for his division. For Stan, it would've been the start he clearly needed.

*Expresses confidence in future actions and direction of the organization:*
Strong project managers know how useful it is to create visual reminders of progress toward milestones or completion. Why? Not just so that people can see the score, but also so that people can build and expand their confidence that the team will hit the mark. When a project begins to go off the rails, so to speak, strong project managers

will take a step back and address the issue, restoring the team's confidence in its progress.

The key here is to be public and to be visible. In Stan's case, he was neither – in fact, he frequently canceled meetings to discuss direction, and was often traveling or unavailable at critical points early in his turnaround effort. Expressing confidence in future actions and directions also requires that you establish a vision in the first place. With that in place, and with evidence of progress (or its lack) coming in regularly, it's much easier to say, "We'll be successful in achieving our customer satisfaction goal by ensuring that our service reps have more streamlined access to all the relevant customer data" or the like.

*Freely and regularly shares strategic business information throughout the organization*

Plans and projects change. That's especially true today in challenging times for businesses of all sizes. Excelling in this element of the "Communicates the Vision" competency gives leaders the flexibility to anticipate, prepare for, and respond to inevitable change. Leaders rarely realize that they don't freely share relevant, strategic business information, but followers frequently report that they feel left out of the loop. So here again we emphasize that it is their experience that matters. Ask them, "what else would you like to know?" "Are you getting enough information to perform well?" Find out what else you can provide, and provide it.

## Empowers

Susan led a business support function responsible for creating a large number of programs that would impact or be attended by most of the executives in a large corporation. She was widely known in her field and considered by many to be a true master of her craft. Susan assembled a small team and met with them frequently, repeatedly emphasizing that all the work coming from the group had to be "world-class." She would direct and personally inspect everyone's work, nearly always in lengthy one-on-one meetings. 90% of the time spent in her staff meetings was dedicated to listening as she held forth.

The model of the team was that of a hub and spokes. Everyone was driven to get their work back to the boss in the form she wanted it. There was little teamwork or collaboration because no one's opinion-except hers - counted. This made the group move very slowly as all items had to flow through the hub creating a bottleneck. At times the boss would discover that two team members had not been collaborating on something and would scold them for this, even though there was little point in collaboration since she would typically veto any idea that was not hers. As a result many innovative ideas were squashed or never vetted. The more devastating result was that few of Susan's planned programs ever came to fruition as she belabored the smallest points of each while the business moved beyond the point where her slow-gestating programs could have been useful.

When people lack the tools or the authority to get their work done, they simply don't get it done. In Susan's case, tools weren't as big an issue as authority – it took Susan's team all of about five days to realize that she would supervise, oversee, and alter everyone's work individually. The team couldn't complete projects simply because Susan had to do all their work for them. Relationships became strained and work suffered in a vicious cycle of diminishing performance.

"Empowerment" is a popular word in business today, particularly in customer-facing environments where people are "empowered" to help customers, frequently it seems by telling them they'll need to fill out a form, call a 1-800 number, or otherwise find someone else to talk to if they want their problem solved. No wonder, then, that the word has lost much of its meaning. In many workplaces, managers are promoted to leadership positions because they are the best at a particular job – and so, being the best salesperson, the best software developer, the best financial analyst, or whatever else, they are asked to supervise the team.

Unfortunately because they are the best in their original role, they typically are forced by circumstance to keep performing that role, and they're asked also to check everyone else's work. The result is a stifling lack of empowerment of the team, and a new manager who is stressed to the breaking point having to perform his former function while usually controlling the work of those around him as well. This serves no one.

Empowerment isn't a highly complicated matter. Truly, it boils down to giving people the tools they need to do their jobs, and giving them the authority they need to make the decisions that are relevant to their roles. A look at the components in this competency helps to clarify.

- Delegates authority and responsibility appropriately
- Supports others in carrying out their responsibilities

*Delegates authority and responsibility appropriately:*
In Susan's case it was clear that while her team was ostensibly responsible for the design and implementation of a variety of programs, no individual member had the authority to design or implement anything. Susan reserved all that authority for herself.

Delegating authority along with responsibility is the key. It's essential for leaders to give their team members the ability to decide and act. Ask your direct reports what they expect to decide and act upon without additional approval. Resolve discrepancies and disputes in this area as quickly as you can. Unless there is a compelling reason why you must make or approve a decision, we recommend strongly that you delegate it.

*Supports others in carrying out their responsibilities:*
Think about the times when people have supported you effectively. Chances are, they didn't hover over your shoulder, check all your work, and second-guess your decisions. Instead, they probably established clear expectations (remember that thing about "Communicates the Vision?") and let you know they had your back if things began to go haywire.

Support can be a tricky area for leaders, especially those new to the leadership game. It's easy to confuse support – the activities and communications that let people know you're on their side and expect them to be successful – with hovering interference. Successful leaders understand how to listen for the kinds of supportive behaviors and communications that will work best for them.

## Fosters Teamwork
- Involves others in planning and decision-making
- Builds cooperative teams in which group members feel valued and empowered and have shared goals
- Attracts and recruits the right people for the right assignments
- Promotes collaboration between functional areas

Think back to the story of Rita, the HR exec who wanted to begin centralizing some HR functions within her company. While Rita had hired a team of people to begin strengthening the corporate HR function in preparation for the centralization, she simultaneously formed a committee of HR leaders from the various business units. Rita took direction from the committee but didn't do a particularly good job of sharing information with her centralized team. When members of that team sought to work with the groups in the business units, they often discovered that Rita and the business unit HR leader had made countervailing agreements or plans.

Rita's frequent changes of direction ended up pitting teams against each other. These changes drove other key people out of the organization altogether. And as you'll recall, when Rita's company was acquired, the news about her leadership style surprised many people, and not at all pleasantly.

The components that make up the "Fosters Teamwork" competency tell the story clearly. One of the most common refrains in bad boss stories is that of the boss who pits people against each other. Sadly, there are many stories of history's leaders who gave two people the same assignment and let them compete for the boss' favor.

*Involves others in planning and decision-making*
Failed leaders hide out in their offices or elsewhere, crafting plans that pit people against one another while they scheme for their own gain. Rarely does the failed leader realize that hiding out and plotting

for his own gain almost certainly assures that he will lose. Think back to communicating the vision, and getting people on board with broad, sweeping goals: the best way to ensure that someone has some "skin in the game" is to involve her in setting the plan for the game in the first place.

*Builds cooperative teams in which group members feel valued and empowered and have shared goals*

In our example with Rita and her human resources team, we found that Rita did a great deal of her work largely in secret. Not only were people left out of decision-making, but they were also left out of work that could have been done collaboratively or at least in the full light of day, so to speak. The result was that people were afraid of her new hires. They felt their opinions and experience were worth little in Rita's eyes. People left the organization frequently, and when they stayed, their cooperation with one another frequently left a great deal to be desired. Successful leaders put their agenda on display and encourage people to work collaboratively, recognizing the contributions of everyone on the team along the way.

*Attracts and recruits the right people for the right assignments*

We are consistently shocked when we see leaders make significant hiring decisions without having candidates spend time with their future teammates. This is as true of staffing internally for projects as it is of hiring from the outside. Successful leaders don't have to be psychics or matchmakers, but they are successful in part because they take the time to build teams on which good relationships can and do form. Not only do they understand the interplay of skills, experience, knowledge, and even personality dynamics, but also they trust and value the input of the people who will actually do the work together.

*Promotes collaboration between functional areas*

In our example with Rita, it was clear that making a change as substantial as centralizing functions that had been created in the individual business units would require a strongly collaborative effort. Rita's heart was clearly in the right place – she wanted to build support for what she knew to be the right thing to do for the company – but her approach left a great deal to be desired. By limiting communication between groups (whether consciously or not), Rita allowed gossip, rumors, and other destructive patterns to take hold. This set up a vicious cycle of declining performance, diminishing collaboration, and growing mistrust. Ultimately, work could not get done in this environment.

Successful leaders recognize that today's environments require teams of teams to work together.

## Not failing is the first step toward success

When we began our study, as we mentioned we were chiefly interested in learning how the most successful leaders in the world got that way. We didn't set out to identify why people fail, but the evidence was so strong we couldn't dare overlook it.

*Failed leaders fail because in the eyes of those around them, they don't communicate a vision for success, they don't empower others to work toward those goals, and they don't foster the kinds of collaborative, cooperative interpersonal and inter-group relationships that make organizations tick.*

As it turns out these three elements are the foundation for leadership success. Weakness in any of these three areas will almost certainly prevent you from reaching your leadership potential. Just as you would first learn how to dribble and shoot if you wanted to be a successful basketball player, you must learn to Communicate the Vision, Empower others, and Foster Teamwork if you are to be a successful leader.

# CHAPTER 2

# THE MAGIC TRIANGLE OF LEADERSHIP SUCCESS

Just as so many people have bad boss stories to share, almost everyone remembers their best boss, or a favorite teacher, coach, or influential mentor. Just as the bad boss stories fall into easily distinguished themes, the great leader stories also reveal common traits.

We set out to understand what separates the best leaders from everyone else, as you know. You also know by now that we discovered, through our study, what separates the *crème de la crème* – the very best leaders in the world – from others in leadership positions, and we also discovered what separates the worst leaders – the *crap de la crap*, if you will – from everyone else too. It turns out that these leaders are indeed quite different, and more importantly, that the differences are predictable, reliable, and measurable.

Of course the results that great leaders cause are measurably different from those caused by poor leaders and there is ample evidence and abundant literature to support that position. There's also your own experience – you know from that experience that when you've worked for the best, you performed better, and when you've worked for the worst... well, if you didn't just leave outright, you probably didn't work to your fullest possible potential even if you did give your fullest effort with utmost honesty.

Great bosses – and great leaders – fascinate nearly everyone. Over the centuries there have been many theories about what makes a great leader. These have ranged from the absurd (height, head size, tone of voice) to the interesting (what is that "charisma" thing all about, anyway?). As you know if you've read many books on leadership, many if not most of these theories are based on one person's experience, or an historical review, and they don't really hold up to the rigors of science. The few studies that attempt some scientific understanding of leadership effectiveness have brought us models of leadership that are highly complex. No one can be expected to perform brilliantly across 21 competencies, each with multiple behavioral elements embedded in them.

When we began our research we had been working with senior as well as junior and mid-level leaders at organizations of many sizes and in multiple industries for years. While we were convinced that the traits shared by the best of these leaders were similar, we knew that our own intuition and our own theories wouldn't advance the cause of leadership science at all. We also sensed that the real keys to success were probably more straightforward than some of the theories advanced thus far would have others believe. Again, though, we didn't yet have the benefit of a scientific study to back up our point of view.

Our study revealed three competencies where the best leaders across all the industries and all the organizations were consistently rated the highest. In each of these competencies, the ratings for the group we call "exemplary leaders" – the best of the best – were substantially, and statistically significantly, higher than all others.

These three competencies are:
**Inspires Confidence**
**Builds Relationships**
**Drives for Results**

Now, if you look at that list of three we're pretty certain that your first reaction will be, "well, of course." Everyone wants to follow someone in whom they have confidence, right? And we've probably had quite strong relationships with our "best boss ever," too. Driving for results seems like a no-brainer, too, doesn't it?

"Inspires Confidence" stood out in our study as the most "important" competency from the standpoint that the exemplary leaders were rated far higher in this area than all others. The gap was bigger here than in any other competency area (for a detailed view of the whole study, see the appendix).

Years ago – during a time when cars had strange appendages called "tailfins" and youngsters engaged in a bizarre ritual known as "playing outside," (it was a decidedly simpler time) one of the authors played football for a championship high school team. The team had such complete confidence in the coach that when they took the field, they actually felt sorry for their opponents. So certain were they that their coach's game plan was superior, and that their preparation was better than everyone else's that they simply felt they *could not lose*. They never did lose during that season. And the coach remains a revered figure, as you would expect.

What's the basis of confidence? To begin, let's take a look at the behavioral dimensions we measured in our study.

***Inspires Confidence***:
- Gains the confidence and trust of others
- Takes responsibility for commitments and actions
- Demonstrates consistency between words and actions

When we think of favored teachers, coaches, bosses, or other mentors, quite often the first thing that comes to mind is our confidence in them, and our trust that they have our mutual best interests in mind. Ask people to tell you their "best boss" stories and you'll probably hear things like, "she just always did the right thing," or "you could count on him to back you up." This is the essence of confidence in others: knowing that you and they are joined in community of interest and effort.

Trust is a critical element of leadership as you know from your own experience. We trust – and build more confidence in – people who "say what they mean and mean what they say," who "walk the talk," whose words and actions align.

At this point you may begin to recognize that the behaviors that make up the "Inspires Confidence" competency create a feedback loop, or a "virtuous circle" in which demonstrating more of the behaviors of "taking responsibility for commitments and actions" leads to better "demonstrating consistency between words and actions," which in turn adds to others' confidence and trust in the leader, and so on.

Many powerful organizational dynamics directly threaten the ability of leaders to inspire confidence, and that is one reason why "best boss" stories are so much less frequent than "worst boss" stories.

Consider that in 2004 and 2005 there were many people across the landscape of financial services who well understood that trouble was brewing in capital markets and in housing. Those who shared their opinion freely about this subject often ran into scorn, ridicule, or worse.

We're not here to rehash excellent research and writing about organizational "defensive routines" or other dynamics. That said it is essential that you recognize this fact: in your efforts to become an exemplary leader, you are absolutely going to run into these routines. The only important question for you as a leader is this: what are you going to do in the face of them?

Here, then, is one of the first tests of your ability to inspire confidence. How capably will you stand for, and act in service of what is right when the pressure is on to do something else?

When we ask this question we ask that you consider it both from the perspective of a subordinate AND from the perspective of a leader. The best bosses – the exemplary leaders – are able to navigate the organization's political maze without compromising their integrity. They are able to "speak truth to power," and do so in a way that preserves or even adds to their own standing in the organization. Even when they don't get their way (for example, to bring about a sea-change in loan underwriting standards during a time when those standards have dropped to the point where it is apparent they are a danger to the organization), these exemplary leaders manage to not imperil their jobs.

Moreover, the truly exemplary leaders inspire confidence by encouraging their followers to speak truth to them. Rather than greeting "bad news" with anger, indifference, derision, or other forms of negativity, exemplary leaders engage. They listen, and they respond with honesty born of an open mind, and dare we say it (we do so dare), an open heart as well. This kind of listening signals to others, "I am not so hard-headed, arrogant, and righteous that I cannot be persuaded of the value of a position different from my own." In other words, this is *responsible listening.*

*Takes responsibility for commitments and actions*

The "responsible listening" we described above stems from being responsible for your commitments and actions. Being responsible means accepting that your decisions and actions are yours. We admire leaders who are willing to say, "I made a mistake," and we equally admire leaders who are willing to say, "Our team's efforts made this happen." Both of these are aspects of responsibility – the recognition that while we may be fallible we are certainly the "author of our own script," so to speak, and also the active willingness to share credit where credit is due.

Consider former President Bill Clinton. Whatever your political beliefs, it is clear that Clinton was revered for his energy, his ability to electrify a crowd with his brilliant oratory, and for his masterful ability to build political coalitions that could press legislation through often turbulent sessions of Congress. Yet Clinton was utterly undone by scandal. While some may see this undoing as the work of a "vast right-wing conspiracy," we argue that Clinton's personal failures, and most particularly his repeated denials of the affair that ultimately brought about his impeachment, did the most damage to his Presidency. Imagine how differently things might have turned out if, during that now infamous press conference in which he wagged his finger and said, "I did not... have sex with that woman..." he had instead said, "you know, I behaved terribly and I have brought pain to my family and shame to myself. I'd like to get to work on repairing the damage I've done to my family, my friends, my associates, and myself."

Since that time we've seen similar failures play out with other politicians – Kwame Kilpatrick, the now-imprisoned former mayor of Detroit, whose political rise was swift and apparently triumphant, was undone by his arrogance and repeated, angry denials of any wrongdoing despite overwhelming evidence. Former financial giants, now disgraced, litter the landscape: Angelo Mozilo of Countrywide, who built a powerhouse lending institution, saw his reputation and precious name destroyed utterly in a matter of a few months. So too with Richard Fuld of Lehman Brothers, Stan O'Neal of Merrill Lynch, John Thain of Merrill, Richard Syron of Freddie Mac, Daniel Mudd of Fannie Mae, James Cayne of Bear Stearns, and many others.

In any one of these cases, these leaders once revered as "masters of the universe" could likely have saved at least their reputations as people of integrity – and thus could have remained leaders whom others would choose to follow – simply by accepting that they in fact bore some responsibility for the conditions their leadership created at their firms. Instead, daily the financial press is bombarded with excuses, blame of others, and examples of astonishingly egregious behavior.

From the perspective of a follower it is easy to understand how a leader who demonstrates being responsible for her commitments and actions inspires our confidence in her. When your boss publicly recognizes you for your efforts, you are appreciative and confident that she will probably do the same thing again in the future. Similarly, when your boss listens to your point of view in a way that demonstrates her engagement and interest, and then explains that the decision or action will not proceed in accordance with your point of view, your confidence rises because you know that she has heard, considered, and understood that point of view.

*Demonstrates consistency between words and actions*

If ever there were a behavior that is utterly self-explanatory, this is it. This is where the rubber meets the road in terms of leadership. This may be the single behavioral element most responsible for the leader's ability to inspire or lose the confidence of others.

Demonstrating consistency between words and actions is as simple as doing what you say, when you say you're going to do it. It includes being honest about the things you're going to do, and the things you're not going to do.

Let's distinguish consistency from rigidity. Everyone understands in a heartbeat that perhaps the most reliable, consistent, repeatable fact of life in organizations is that things change. Projects are redirected, accelerated, or canceled. Acquisitions come and go. Political regimes change. Milestones, objectives, or requirements are discovered anew or the conditions underlying them change.

The leader's ability to communicate the nature of change and its impact on systems, processes, tools, activities, and behaviors is an essential asset in inspiring confidence and in leadership more broadly defined as well. Demonstrating consistency between words and actions frequently means being able and willing quickly to "stand up" in front of your followers to announce, "We're going to be doing this differently in the future," or "We're not going to do X even though I said we'd do X, and the reason is Y."

### Builds Relationships

A major manufacturingcenter for a national business had numerous reports of employee discontent. The ER surveys showed the majority of a population of more than 1500 people had significant morale issues. Some of these had to do with scheduling problems, some had to do with inconsistent performance management practices, lack of training, impersonal attitudes by leadership, and even some hints of discrimination.

These issues were surfaced in a major survey. However, some of the problems involved the director of the facility – call her Judy.

Judy's leadership style could be described as a hard-charging, "take the hill" type of attitude. She demanded complete loyalty. She had a tendency to hire according to her own likeness making her immediate direct-report team of Junior Directors seem like her clones to others in the facility.

She also isolated herself. Comments on the surveys indicated that some of the 1200 staff members had never seen her in the two-plus years that the facilityhad been running. She had a reputation of managing upward very well. Many of the staff felt that she only came out of her office when the more senior leaders came into the facilityto visit.

Judy's career was in jeopardy even though in her mind, she was ready for promotion and felt that she was promised this after the successful start-up of this facility.

Rather than allow these attitudes to fester, the company decided to take action. Judy was a valuable and successful leader at least by the numbers. The senior leaders decided to attempt to salvage the situation.

First, Judy's boss shared the results of the Employee Relations survey with her and made it clear that the issues had to be resolved.

Then, we began a teambuilding campaign that included:
- 360 Feedback for the Director and all her Junior Directors (JDs).
- Individual coaching sessions allowed the Director and each JD to understand the primary messages of the feedback and to create individual development plans.
- A group roll up of data on all the JDs along with thematic comments from raters was presented to the Director and her JD group.
- The Director and JD team took the group results and:

  o *Met over these to identify common actions that would attack the primary issues on the ER Survey and the 360 data*
  o *Each JD met with their own teams to review their personal development plans and get more feedback on these plans.*
  o *The Director led a presentation to the entire supervisory staff about these results, her own feedback and action plan and the plan from the JD Group.*

We ensured that follow-up work was well in place.

Additionally, Judy moved her office from an isolated position in the structure to the middle of the center. She built a glass office so everyone could see her. She put into effect an open door policy – anyone could come in with a knock on the door.

She walked the center once per day to meet ad hoc with staff. She had skip-level meetings weekly until each staff member had time with her. She instituted and encouraged occasional, informal teambuilding events on-site.

Two years later:
- ♦ Discrimination claims disappeared
- ♦ Moralescores on∂ the survey improved significantly
- ♦ The Junior Director Leaders improved their trust level with their supervisor staff
- ♦ The facility led the nation in all seven key performance measures
- ♦ The Director was cited for instituting best practices in both performance and personnel management practices.

Obviously, Judy put a lot of effort into building relationships, and into building trust (they go together nicely, don't they?). The effort clearly paid off for Judy and for her group, department, and organization. Let's break it down a bit.

## Builds Relationships
- Treats others fairly and with respect
- Develops positive work relationships with higher management, peers, direct reports, and external constituencies

At the outset of our work with Judy, it was clear that she believed strongly that she treated others fairly and with respect. However, many of her followers simply didn't see it that way. They resented her driving style, her inaccessibility, and her apparent unwillingness to surround herself with people who seemed different at all. While none of these elements in and of themselves sunk Judy or her relationships, taken together they made it difficult for others to experience her as anything other than aloof, insensitive, and even discriminatory. Judy's subordinates in some cases felt disrespected.

Until Judy could see this in black-and-white, others' experience of her was a blind spot. She saw the results of the unit and felt strongly (and even rightly) that those were "her" results, and they should speak for themselves. When she saw the ER survey and more importantly her 360-degree feedback results, Judy understood immediately that she wouldn't continue getting those kinds of results for long if she didn't make some big, visible, and important changes.

It's critical also to understand that successfully building relationships means building them across the board – with higher management, peers, subordinates, and others. At the outset of her journey Judy recognized that her focus on building relationships with higher management and select peers had alienated others. This moment of recognition was essential to her ability to change course.

### Drives for Results

We consulted to a group that performed telesales for a large, high tech organization. They were part of a system of sales groups across the US. Tom, the leader of this team (housing about 300 people) was roundly criticized for underachieving. For about two years running, Tom's team had been near the bottom of sales when compared to the other regions against which his team was measured.

In addition, this team had problems with recruiting phone representatives. There were three levels of leadership and the second level neither worked well together nor did they trust each other. For a small second level team, this behavior was noticeable. In fact, people referred to it as "the war."

After we collected 360-degree feedback on the leadership, we helped them structure development plans. As you might expect, we put the two most contentious leaders on a track of relationship-building for themselves.

Next, we provided them a review of the leader team profile. On a group level, the results demonstrated the core problems they were experiencing. As part of our process we also interviewed many supervisors and representatives to get an understanding of their view of the leadership team's strengths and weaknesses.

The interviews provided clear feedback to the team that the war between the second level leaders was having a strong negative impact on the supervisors and the representatives. This data reinforced to these two leaders how important it was to carry through on their individual plans.

In addition, the top leader of the facility was perceived to be a poor communicator, particularly with respect to the group's goals and direction. The 360 data and interviews indicated that skills involving managing change were lacking. The group had no idea how it was going to improve its performance. It did not have a clear picture of what was expected. It had little faith that this leadership team could create positive change.

The team identified a number of initiatives that they would undertake together to turn these perceptions around.

♦ The warring individuals committed to managing their differences privately and with tools we provided during training in conflict management.

♦ The leader team drafted a clear plan communicating the strategy and tactics they would use to make the necessary changes/improvements in performance. The team set a goal to become the best-performing sales unit among all the regional centers.

♦ Clear expectations and measures were provided to each employee.

♦ Coaching was installed for each member on a regular basis to improve their individual performance. This was not done in the past, although training on basic skills had been provided.

♦ Rewards, verbal and otherwise, were created on a team basis for outstanding performance by individuals and teams. Employee teams had direct input into team level rewards.

♦ Quarterly reviews of progress were provided so the measures could be clearly seen by all employees.

♦ Supervisors were empowered to make decisions that previously needed approval from above.

These were some of the initiatives. They evolved over a two year period as team dynamics changed and as growth in the business progressed.

Over an 18 month period the shift in performance for this sales group was dramatic. The chart below shows the improvement in the

360 results during that time period. Each of 19 competencies improved. Change Management was the most dramatic.

The sales improvements – the results that the leaders were driving for – are below:

- ◆ Sales productivity increased by 17%
- ◆ Sales productivity per employee was the highest of all centers
- ◆ Total sales revenue was the highest of all region sales groups.
- ◆ Employee turnover was reduced by 9%

## Communication Fortune 50 Sales Call Center Team Leadership Behavior Change – 360 Feedback

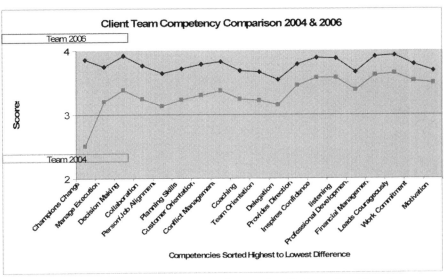

What you will likely notice most about the Drives for Results competency is how closely interdependent it is with other competencies. When we look at the behaviors individually, here's what we find:

### Drives for results
- • Possesses high internal work standards and sets ambitious, yet attainable goals
- • Persists in the face of adversity
- • Unhesitatingly makes decisions as required

It is easy for leaders to fall into the trap of thinking that driving for results requires being a hard-driving, take-no-prisoners kind of leader who badgers, pushes relentlessly, and berates others when things don't go his way. It may be the word "drives" in the Drives for Results competency that gives people this impression.

Whatever it is, don't be fooled: our research reveals that successfully achieving long term results is so highly correlated with building relationships that it is virtually impossible for a leader to achieve results without having strong, positive relationships. While correlation is not the same as cause, in this case it is almost as if success in relationship-building gives rise to profitability.

As a department head for a boutique consulting firm, Alicia was as close as anyone could get to being made a full partner. She was highly successful by virtually any measure: she had a stable of high-dollar clients, routinely engaging them for increasingly complex work.

Despite her impressive credentials, Alicia could sense that the president of the firm wasn't going to "pull the trigger" on making her a partner and she found it increasingly frustrating. Alicia scheduled a meeting with him during which she planned to threaten to leave the firm and take her clients with her to a major competitor unless he offered her a partnership on the spot.

Instead of a confrontation, though, Alicia got a surprise in that meeting. Ted, the president, sat in the conference room with all the other partners. He asked Alicia to talk about her relationships with each one. Alicia spoke about how much she liked, and how well she worked with, each of the partners. She referenced deals on which they had collaborated, shared efforts to lure big clients into the firm, and clients they had groomed and developed together.

Then Ted asked Alicia to talk about the trainees she had worked with, grooming them to become full consultants at the firm. At this point, she became less comfortable: all but two of the nine trainees assigned to Alicia had left the firm. Five of those seven were now rising through the ranks at competing companies. Alicia revealed in that meeting that a current trainee had just given his notice. Ted shared that although displays of anger were still common, Alicia's reputation as a "screamer" was killing her with her trainees.

Through an increasingly discomfiting two-hour meeting, Alicia, Ted, and the agency partners delved deeply into her relationships inside the company as well as "around town." Alicia learned that she was frequently perceived as unresponsive, aloof, and haughty. In a rare moment of vulnerability, Alicia revealed that when she herself was a trainee, she had cultivated these attitudes to appear tough. What served her well at times back then, though, had become a weakness. Though her clients were firmly committed to her, few others in the company, or among her clients, felt she was so indispensible. Alicia understood clearly in this moment that she would have to broaden her base of relationships, and make those relationships stronger, more authentic, and more durable, if she was going to create the kind of lasting results that would bring her a partnership.

Alicia worked tirelessly to build these relationships. She changed her style with her trainees, remaining demanding and clear about expectations but quite noticeably stopping her once-frequent tirades. She started a habit of taking twice-daily "random walks" through the offices to talk to assistants, trainees, and young consultants, as well as others. While some people – Alicia too – found this a bit awkward in the first week, soon it became more comfortable. As Alicia followed up with answers to their questions or responses to their requests, she noticed that people inside and outside the organization began to seek her advice and help. Calls that previously had been difficult became easier. In the following year, Alicia nearly doubled her prior year's revenue. When she sat down with Ted to get her bonus he handed her the impressive check and a partnership agreement to sign as well.

Alicia – already outstanding in a business driven almost entirely by successful relationships – spent a year focused on building stronger relationships. At the end of that year, the results she produced spoke for themselves. This is an example of the incredibly tight correlation between "Builds Relationships" and "Drives for Results." One may not truly cause the other, but the data show convincingly that the people who are great achievers of results are almost always those who build the strongest, deepest, broadest pool of successful relationships.

Exemplary Leaders are rare. This rarity has led people to believe, perhaps for centuries, that great leaders are born that way and that their leadership skills are an expression of innate talents. Our research shows that in fact people can learn to be highly effective, even Exemplary Leaders.

The "secret" to being an Exemplary Leader is no secret at all. First, you must not fail in the three areas in the "Tragic Triangle:" Communicates the Vision, Fosters Teamwork, and Empowers. If you do those three things at least reasonably well then you will have established the foundation for leadership success. With that foundation in place, you will build stronger relationships and you will see that your relationships support your ability to drive effectively for results. Then, as your relationships pay off in the delivery of results, you will profit from the virtuous circle of Inspiring Confidence, Building (yet stronger) Relationships, and Driving for (yet better) Results.

# CHAPTER 3

# THE GOLDEN TRIANGLE OF EXEMPLARY LEADERSHIP

Thus far we've seen that the worst leaders get that way because they fail to Communicate the Vision, Foster Teamwork, and Empower those around them. We've also seen that the best leaders are so highly regarded because they Inspire Confidence, Build Relationships, and Drive for Results. These six competencies form the essential core of leadership effectiveness. The reason why these are the core is quite simple: all six work together to form what we have come to call the Golden Triangle of Exemplary Leadership.

The path to success in leadership is a lot like the path to success in other endeavors. It starts with learning and becoming skilled at the fundamentals. Another way to look at it is that the path to being good starts with not failing. Think about it: if you can't dribble a basketball, it's difficult to play at all. If you are a poor dribbler, you can play but it's hard to play well – defenders will easily steal the ball and you'll soon find your teammates trying to keep you from having to dribble at all.

So it is in leadership: if you can't do the basics at all, you won't lead. If you do the basics poorly, you'll fail as a leader and your "teammates" will soon remove you from leadership positions, or they will work harder to isolate and insulate you from your own failures. It's easy to see that neither of these are good outcomes.

Our research shows that the best leaders in the world are known more than anything else for their ability to inspire confidence. This competency rises above all others in the profiles of the best leaders by significant amounts. In fact, it is possible to argue that the ability to inspire others to be confident of you is the "true north" of great leadership. It's painfully clear, though, that no one can gain the confidence of others simply by going out and asking for it. This kind of confidence is earned.

It's true: there are specific behavioral elements that we measure to "roll up" to the Inspires Confidence competency. These behaviors have to do generally with "walking the talk." Without question, these "integrity" measures are critically important to inspiring the confidence of others. Yet there's more to having the confidence of others than doing just these things.

We know this because we've tracked the correlations of competencies within the model. Correlation is simple – it's the relationship between two variables. So, for example, we almost always see "Drives for Results" and "Builds Relationships" move together. In fact, these are the most highly correlated competencies in our study. Their relationship is so close that it is almost perfect (see the appendix for the details of the study including a chart of correlations). It is almost impossible to achieve results – and to be perceived broadly as someone who gets results – without having excellent relationships.

The next highest correlations all involve the "Tragic Triangle" competency cluster. All of these three are also so highly correlated with each other that they almost always move in tandem. Interestingly, "Communicates the Vision," which is highly correlated with both "Fosters Teamwork" and "Empowers," is also highly correlated with "Builds Relationships," "Drives for Results," and "Inspires Confidence."

Now that we've bombarded you with a fair dose of statistical findings, here's some help in understanding what to do with them.

In essence, the two parts of our model come together like this: the leadership fundamentals of Communicates the Vision, Fosters Teamwork, and Empowers form the legs or sides of the Golden Triangle – the stable base from which the triangle is formed. Where these legs meet, the traits of Exemplary Leaders emerge as the triangle's points: Inspires Confidence, Builds Relationships, and Drives for Results.

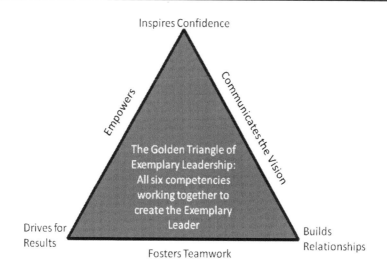

To improve your leadership effectiveness, start by improving your ability to communicate the vision. What is it you and the team you lead are seeking to accomplish? How can you make that clearer, more engaging, more relevant? How can you help others understand the link between what they do and the organization's larger goals?

By improving how others experience your leadership in this area of Communicating the Vision, you are almost guaranteed to improve how they experience you in terms of Fostering Teamwork and Empowering others.

More importantly, you are also almost guaranteed to achieve better results, to have stronger relationships, and to inspire their confidence to a higher degree as well.

We're convinced that one reason why leaders of all kinds like to use sports analogies is because they make the vision of success so clear. In every major sport we're aware of, the vision is straightforward: win. The path to victory is equally straightforward: score better than your opponent. Since sports have definitive, binary outcomes (win or lose) and since they typically have visible scoreboards (it's 14-3 with 10 minutes left in the 4th quarter of a football game), the vision is broadly communicated and there's precious little room for misunderstanding at least at the macro level.

Since sports make it easy, consider taking a lesson from your favorite sporting event and applying it to your own leadership situations. Take a short inventory of the ways you've communicated about what it means to "win" in your organization. Do people know what winning means? Do they know what winning an individual "game" looks like? Do they have a clear picture of the "season?" Can you help them to understand what it means to make the "playoffs," or win the "championship?"

If you can do these things and check in with everyone under the umbrella of your leadership to see if they understand these things in the same way, you're well on your way to communicating a clear, effective vision of the future. As our study shows, it's highly likely that you will then be on your way to winning your own game of becoming an exemplary leader.

Our research has shown what many people understand intuitively: a leader with great relationship skills gets better results. As we've said the research reveals a startlingly high correlation between "Builds Relationships" and "Drives for Results" – a relationship that is so strong, in fact, that without one, the other is virtually impossible to achieve.

This has incredibly powerful implications for people seeking to become exemplary leaders. You'll remember that being known for a powerful "Drive for Results" is a key hallmark of the best leaders. Yet think of how many of those bad boss stories involve people who confuse being driven with being stern taskmasters.

For much of the 20th century, people thought that those under their leadership didn't want to work very hard, that they had to be controlled, forced to work long hours, and that their output had to be closely monitored. This notion formed the core of many management philosophies and much of management education. It is so deeply ingrained in our culture that many people still believe it, or even if they don't believe it, they still behave as if they do.

This is why so many bad boss stories involve things like people being told to schedule the birth of their children at times when there's less business impact, or to cancel a trip to a grandparent's funeral because "it's just so busy right now," or similarly egregious examples. Leaders who make these kinds of bizarre, inappropriate, or simply inhumane demands would probably rate themselves quite highly in the area of "driving for results." What they see when they look at that competency, after all, is the word "drive." To drive for results, they reason, must mean driving particularly hard, being known for being "driven," and hey, if you happen to drive a few people insane, or drive a few dozen talented people out of the company, well, that's just part of the game.

Stop here and consider the impact of a failing leader whose behavior drives people out of her organization. Remember Judy, the call center leader who turned around her failing relationships and re-energized her career? Prior to her personal turnaround, three of Judy's Junior Directors had resigned their positions for roles in other companies. Not only did these people's departure cost Judy's company the time and expense of hiring replacements, the departures also created ripple effects. Institutional knowledge left with those people. Their direct reports lost productivity as did their subordinate teams. Judy's reputation suffered as she was increasingly perceived as someone who couldn't hold on to top talent.

It is routinely estimated that the cost of replacing managers ranges between 1 and 3 times their annual salary. However, these estimates are only of direct costs for recruiting and bringing the new managers up to productivity. Less frequently considered, and typically more costly, are the ancillary costs of the lost productivity of other members of the organization.

Think also about who typically leaves an organization voluntarily. Usually, the people who opt out of a bad situation first are the people who have the most options. Who has the most options to take a different job? Not the weak performers. No, it's usually the top talent that goes first if the leader isn't up to the task of retaining them. Even if it's not your superstar who leaves, perhaps you will find, after enough people have bolted out the door that those folks you thought of as "solid citizens" were worth a lot more to the organization than you originally believed.

Exemplary leaders do more than understand that clarity of vision and solid relationships matter. They create these visions and work hard to build these relationships. Our research shows that these two competencies – Communicates the Vision, and Builds Relationships – have incredibly strong influence in a leaders' overall effectiveness. Exemplary leaders build on this knowledge by ensuring that the people around them understand the vision, goals, and expectations. They also ensure that their relationships with the people around them are strong, two-way exchanges of value. While this seems to come naturally to some people, our research and experience shows clearly that these behaviors can be learned, and that people can and do build strength and skill in these areas with time and effort.

Exemplary leaders understand intuitively that results today are a function of unlocking the best and highest motivations of those around them. First and foremost that means recognizing the dignity, humanity, and talent of the people around them. It means recognizing that people who understand and buy in to a particular vision, and who have the tools and authority they require to accomplish an objective, typically will put forward honest, substantial effort to achieve it.

Take a quick second look at the paragraph above and you will see the bones of the entire "Tragic Triangle" competency group represented: people who understand and buy in to a vision, and who have the tools and authority to achieve it… right there, you see "Communicates the Vision" and "Empowers." In addition you'll note that these are people who are working in organizations, with others. Enter "Fosters Teamwork."

Now, add strong, respectful relationships to the mix and you have the ingredients for highly effective leadership. It would be tempting to say that results will take care of themselves, but we all know that's not the case at all. Being known for possessing high internal work standards, confident decision-making, and for persistence in the face of adversity all feature in the "Drives for Results" competency. Imagine how you would be viewed by others in this area if you had poor relationships, and you can sense intuitively the basis for the correlation between "Builds Relationships" and "Drives for Results."

Recall also that the "Drives for Results" competency includes the element "possesses high internal work standards." Clearly, what this means is that people who drive effectively for results get a lot done themselves. Think about your good boss and bad boss stories again and it probably won't take you long to recognize that the best bosses shoulder their share of the burden, or that the worst bosses shrugged off more responsibility than they should have.

This goes directly to "walking the talk," doesn't it? Now, think again about the Inspires Confidence competency, which has almost entirely to do with demonstrating consistency between words and actions and gaining the trust and confidence of others. Imagine for a moment trying to inspire the confidence of others, or being perceived as someone who demonstrates consistency between words and actions, if you as a leader are unable or unwilling to "do your part." Pretty obvious, isn't it?

Our study took us on a journey of discovery about leadership. We started out looking for what made great leaders great. Along the way, we discovered that the great leaders shared common traits, and set themselves apart from others by Inspiring Confidence, Building Relationships, and Driving for Results. We also found that Failed Leaders distinguished themselves, though not in the way they probably wanted to. These Failed Leaders failed most in common areas too. They failed to Communicate the Vision, Foster Teamwork, and Empower others. As we continued our "tour" of leadership, we found the correlations between these competencies to be so incredibly strong that they are utterly undeniable. There is no question, based on our research, that these six competencies work together, and that several of them – notably "Builds Relationships" and "Communicates the Vision," serve as strong levers, influencing people's experience of the leader as a whole in remarkably powerful ways.

What we found in these correlations and in the study of these thousands of leaders is that most often the Exemplary leaders and Failed Leaders are distinguished by strongly differing philosophies of leadership.

### *Your Philosophy of Leadership Matters*

The fast-rising President and Chief Operating Officer of a fast-growing technology company, Rick had an abiding reputation as a ferociously-driven, hot-tempered, brilliant man who remembered every detail that was ever presented to him.  He presided over every significant operational review meeting, and the books presented to him in these meetings were legendary across the organization for their depth of detail.  Nothing was too trivial or inconsequential, it seemed, to escape Rick's incredible focus and demand for transaction-level knowledge.  Woe betide the executive who answered, "I don't know, I'll have to find out and get back to you" to any question Rick posed.  Rick was known to excoriate these executives publicly and with extraordinary vitriol.  He ruled by fear.

Rick spent about nine days of every month personally closing the monthly books through these business review meetings and through individual review.  His philosophy of leadership was to "do it all himself," and to constantly review and rehash the work of his subordinates.  As a result, these executives built large organizations whose sole focus was preparing the incredibly detailed reporting Rick demanded.  More importantly, because these executives were terrified of what might happen to them if they made a decision Rick didn't like, they felt forced to review every detail of their own organizations as rigorously as Rick did.  Their subordinate mangers cascaded this authoritarian, detail-driven, disempowering style throughout the company.

This leadership style fostered highly bureaucratic business units with many functions that seemed hidebound.  Attempts to improve processes or create innovative products were snuffed out before they could make it to Rick's office, typically because no one wanted to go to Rick's office with an idea that required speculation or that rested on a business case that might be subject to scrutiny.

Although this institution was highly successful for a time, when margins began to shrink even as revenue grew, Rick found it impossible to cut costs quickly enough to salvage the company – the enormous bureaucracies and rigid silos that had built over time simply could not be made more efficient fast enough.  Business-unit leaders had never learned how to decide, act, and execute without calling on Rick first. Ultimately the company was acquired and Rick was cast out of the newly combined organization. So too were many senior managers, especially those who had spent whole careers with the company, who had never learned how to lead large organizations.

Rick's philosophy of leadership clearly impacted this company. While no one would question that Rick had intense drive for results, his focus was more on the drive than the results. Rick's intensive scrutiny and his breathtaking recall and knowledge of minute details were at one point almost certainly a strength for him, but as the company grew, and as the complexity of its challenges grew, what was once a strength became Rick's weakness. Few highly senior, seasoned executives who joined the company and who could have led substantial change, wanted to stay – they found they had no authority to act, and their relationships with Rick quickly became strained.

Contrast this inward-turning, numbers- and details-focused philosophy of leadership with that of Adrienne, the President of a European manufacturing company we worked with. Adrienne's company had also grown dramatically, from a group of just a few hundred to nearly 8,000 people spread across multiple sites. As the company grew, Adrienne asked her senior leadership to focus on ensuring that everyone in every role knew exactly how they fit into the company's plans – and her own plans – for continued success and growth.

Adrienne plotted out a chart that showed all the company's goals, and overlaid it on an organization chart. She used colored lines to show which teams were responsible for accomplishing which goals. When the chart was done, anyone in the organization could quite easily see how their work "rolled up" to a goal that was important to the company president.

Adrienne posted these charts in every one of the company's facilities. She made regular visits to the facilities and spent time walking the floor of each shop and office to ask people for feedback on their experience of working at the company. Adrienne's executives and managers routinely did the same, reporting the results up to her at regular intervals.

49

Adrienne and Rick had two markedly different philosophies of leadership – not just styles, but in fact, core beliefs about what a leader does – and these differing philosophies led them to behave in utterly divergent ways. Rick spent most of his time in his own office, only rarely leaving the headquarters to visit other corporate facilities. Adrienne, on the other hand, relied almost exclusively on her mobile phone, a laptop, and the company's travel agent – she spent so much time out in the field that her assistant joked about having forgotten what she looked like.

Neither of these philosophies is right or wrong. There is no question that exemplary leaders generally favor the latter, outward-facing, relationship, vision, and empowerment-oriented philosophy. Leaders who are inward-turning, operationally-focused tacticians can become exemplary leaders too – but they must work extra hard to ensure that they pay substantial attention to relationships, to visibility, and to communicating a vision and trusting those around them to fulfill it.

# CHAPTER 4

## CHANGING THE WAY YOU CHANGE

Well, here we are. You've taken the self-assessment at the beginning of the book, and you've seen and built some understanding of your results. You've learned why Failed Leaders fail, and what makes Exemplary Leaders different from all the rest of us mere mortals. And we're betting you've done what most people do: you've probably started looking at the gaps formed by your self assessment results and the measures of the Magic Triangle. You've started to think about how you can inspire others to be more confident in your leadership, how you can build stronger, better relationships, and how you can more effectively drive for results.

These are all great things to think about but there's still a chance that tackling these things first and foremost will get you nowhere, fast. Let's face it: change is hard. We know that's a terrible cliché but we also know it to be utterly true, since we're three guys who have made, like so many other people, many attempts to change behavior only to see them come up woefully short. Our argument is simple: if you are going to invest the time and energy to change your behavior and make that change stick over the long haul, you want to be sure that your investment has a better-than-average chance of paying off.

So we're going to take some time here to talk about change from two fronts. First, how is that people really and truly come to a point where they change behavior, and make that change hold up through the inevitable pressures that creep into life? Second, we'll share the time-tested, research-proven ways to plot a course of behavior change that will pay off with measurable and meaningful results.

Now to be fair these are two highly separate matters. It's important to understand them both, though, and to understand them in this sequence because change, as we said (and as you know) is hard. It's hard to do in the first place, and it's even harder to do well.

John was the kind of manager who liked to be, as he put it, "closely involved." His direct reports referred to this involvement with less-flattering terms like "micromanagement" and "soul-crushing perfectionism," but John believed that it was important to ensure that everything was, well, perfect.

It was starting to get a bit tougher for John as his boss called him to attend higher-level meetings and take on more responsibility. John needed his team, but his team's performance was slipping. The harder he pressed for perfection, the more frequently people left, and the more he found himself sweating out 14-hour days in his office. Before long even that kind of effort wasn't enough.

John had a 360-degree feedback assessment and was astonished at the results. He knew he wasn't considered an empowering manager, but until the coaching session we had with him, he had never seen the relationship between empowerment and the rest of the Golden Triangle competencies. He didn't understand until then that his insistence on inspecting his team's work was undermining his relationships with them, and preventing them from producing at their highest level.

When the light went on for John, it really went on. At first he was deeply, even profoundly upset. He told us with high emotion, "this really has to change." Something's gotta give here; I'm losing good people, and I'm losing touch with my family because I'm constantly working. This can't go on."

John also saw in that session that he didn't have a model for how to be an empowering manager. But he did have a strategic and tactical mind, so he put together a plan and started working it. He canvassed his peers and direct reports, soliciting their input about how better to empower others. He made his development goals and plans public and invited others to help him remain accountable and on track toward his goals.

It took some time but John's plan worked. He stopped inspecting every single piece of work, and handed decision-making authority to his team in a number of areas. By doing this, he freed up time to concentrate on the new responsibilities his boss wanted him to tackle. More importantly, he restored his relationships with his team and at home as well.

We didn't tell John about it at the time, but he did three very particular things especially well through this process. His story illustrates the three absolutely essential conditions that research shows must be in place before anyone will make a behavior change that has any realistic probability of holding up to the test of time. These three elements are:

1. The crystallization of discontent
2. A focal event
3. Follow-up and follow-through

The crystallization of discontent is that moment of realization that one must change no matter what. It's the moment when you say to yourself, "I will do anything to stop X from happening again." For John, this moment came when he was looking at his 360 results and seeing in black-and-white that his team was deeply dissatisfied and ready to leave.

Having coached thousands of people through the 360-degree feedback process we can tell you with absolute certainty that reading what your peers and direct reports really think of you can definitely crystallize your discontent. Of course, there is another possible reaction – you can just deny what you're seeing. We'll come back to that later.

A focal event comes about when someone or something shows you the way to move forward. For John, this focal event came during our coaching session when he began to see how the competency of "empowers" is related to the rest of the Golden Triangle competencies. This insight led John to start thinking not just about *what* to change, but more importantly, *how to change it*. Where the crystallization of discontent might give you that pit-in-your-stomach sense of gloom, the focal event shows you that you *can* change. It's a bit like being out on a hike in the wilderness and thinking that you're hopelessly lost, and then opening up your map and seeing right where you are.

Lastly you absolutely must have regular follow-up and follow-through. Many of us have tried over time to lose weight, for example, or to learn a language, play an instrument, become better golfers, and so on. Weight loss is perhaps the best example of the importance of follow-up and follow-through simply because it is the easiest to grasp. We understand in an instant, intuitively, that if we give up our new way of eating and exercising, we'll fall easily back into old patterns and our goal will be lost. So it is with any other behavior – if you want to master it, you must practice it routinely and you must have structures in place that will keep you from backsliding and returning to familiar patterns.

John saved himself the pain of backsliding by getting others involved in his development plans. He went public, telling his team what he had seen, what he intended to change, and how he planned to do it. Same with his colleagues and his manager – they were all in on the plan. John's public stance boxed him in, as it were – it would've been pretty embarrassing to fall back into old patterns knowing that everyone he was working with knew that he was committed to change them. The simple action of making his plans public helped John get started in the follow up and follow through arena. He also scheduled routine feedback meetings with peers and direct reports, as well as with his manager, and had a follow-up 360-degree feedback assessment the next year.

We're pleased to say that John's scores rose significantly between the first and second 360. We're even more pleased to report that John's career growth continued, and he spent more time with his family as well.

The crystallization of discontent, a focal event, and follow up and follow through. When these three conditions are in place, your efforts to change your behavior have a much better chance of sticking. If any of them are missing, it's going to be a much harder row to hoe.

As you might expect, people do a lot to avoid that moment of crystallization of discontent. After all, it's not fun. Here are some of the most common reactions we've gotten over the years when we've sat down with people to review feedback and create a development plan.

> ➢ The wrong people filled out the surveys
> ➢ My job makes me act this way; I'm not really like that
> ➢ Some of my respondents have it in for me
> ➢ The computer must have scored this wrong
> ➢ I used to be this way but I've changed recently
> ➢ My boss gave me low scores because he/she doesn't like me
> ➢ This was just a bad time to do this
> ➢ My manager asked me to act this way; I'm actually nicer
> ➢ My peers are just jealous of my success
> ➢ I purposefully picked people who don't like me
> ➢ It's all accurate, but I just don't care

We have heard every one of these things, and many more, in our work with managers and executives. Justification, rationalization, and denial are legitimate reactions to feedback – in fact, these are probably the most common reactions to feedback. The fact that they are common does not mean that they are useful. If you are interested in becoming an Exemplary Leader, you must be willing to accept feedback, and act on it.

Recall what we said at the beginning of the book: Leadership only exists in the experience of the people around the leader. We have long found it fascinating that people who claim to be interested in developing themselves are so quick to reject information that is perhaps the most direct expression of other people's experience of their leadership.

### Figuring out what to change... as well as how to change it

Knowing how to change – or at least what has to be in place in order to give you a chance of being successful in changing – is one thing. But there's another critical piece of the puzzle. What do you change? How can you determine with meaningful confidence which changes will truly have an impact?

Consider the story of three students, Harley, Allison, and Keith. All three are sophomores in high school. Harley is a solid student with an A- average. Allison is a passable student with a C+ average. Keith is on the verge of flunking out. Now, imagine that all of these students get better, all by about the same percentage amount (another way to say this is that they each undertake a successful program of behavior change). Harley goes from being a strong student to an outstanding, top-of class pupil. Allison goes from the C+ to the B or perhaps B+ range, and Keith goes from flunking out to perhaps a C- or D+ range, but at least now he is passing.

As you can see, the same percentage change for each of these three students has a remarkably different impact. In Harley's case, she has moved from being a student who probably could've gotten into some very good schools to being one who can more likely be accepted to one of the top schools. Keith was in real danger of failing entirely but can now in all likelihood continue on and get a diploma. Allison, on the other hand, has made the same effort and made the same percentage change as the others but has relatively less to show for it in terms of results of the change.

### Crossing the Cusps

The essential lesson here is to focus on the changes that will have the greatest impact. Those "high impact" points are what we call the "cusps" in our leadership study. Crossing one of these significant points – either by climbing above the 10th percentile in a significantly flawed competency or by moving from good to great by getting higher than the 80th percentile – has a greater impact in terms of your overall effectiveness than does moving from, say, the 45th to the 70th percentile in a given area.

Think about it this way: if you are in the bottom 10% of your peer group in a given competency, that's an area where you, frankly, are failing. In the LSI report that you should have in front of you if you've taken the assessment prior to reading this book, you'll note that we refer to these weaknesses as areas where you are "challenged." Correcting that behavior takes you from "flunking out" (truly, perhaps even losing your job) to a point where you are at least passable. If you are rated as challenged in one of the "Tragic Triangle" competencies of Communicates the Vision, Fosters Teamwork, or Empowers, then you without question must address that issue immediately, or you risk failing entirely as a leader.

Similarly, if you find yourself ranked in, say, the 78th percentile in a given competency area, and you raise that rating to, for example, the 85th percentile, there is a very good chance that you will be seen as one of the "go-to people" in that area. In the LSI report, we refer to this higher cusp as "Exemplary." Competencies in which you find yourself nearing an "Exemplary" rating are worth noting as potentially key areas for building on strengths. Crossing the Exemplary cusp is an opportunity to turn an area in which you are already quite good into a career-making super-strength.

Changing your own behavior is a difficult task and one that is fraught with pitfalls. We are, after all, creatures of habit and it is not easy to alter our habits. If you're over the age of about 35 and have ever tried to lose weight and keep it off you will know that it's not as simple as just saying, "I'm going to get back in shape." So, when it comes to changing your leadership behavior, you naturally want to take an approach that is more likely to bear fruit than to be a waste of time. After all, if you're doing this for the right reasons, you're doing it because you want the people around you to have a better experience of your leadership.

Because it is difficult to change, it's important to go about changing in a way that has the highest expected chance of success. Success in this case means change that has a meaningful impact on your performance as a leader. So now you have two dimensions from which to think about how to approach change: The Golden Triangle of Exemplary Leadership, with its six highly-correlated competency areas, and this model of crossing the cusps.

If you take yet another look at your assessment results you will probably see some areas that approach a cusp. We're hopeful that these will be areas where you're on the verge of entering the 80th or higher percentile, but if not, that's okay too as your starting point will be that much clearer. Start by identifying all those competency areas where you have a chance to cross a significant cusp. Now, align those with the Golden Triangle. Remember especially that you must perform well in the Tragic Triangle Competencies of Communicates the Vision, Fosters Teamwork, and Empowers in order to have a chance to become an exemplary leader. If you are failing in any of those areas, you must address those first. If you have the chance to cross over into the 80th or higher percentile in one of those areas, it's useful to include it in your development plan.

Remember also that you must have the three building blocks of successful change in place too: the crystallization of discontent, a focal event, and follow-up and follow-through, in order to have a chance at successfully maintaining the behavior change over the long haul.

The crystallization of discontent may be a relatively easy thing to achieve – in our coaching we have seen hundreds of people who are shocked by their 360-degree feedback results, and many quite unpleasantly so. We structure our coaching sessions so that they provide that focal event; the event that points the way forward and that creates a roadmap to successful behavior change. Follow-up and follow-through, in our opinion, is the hardest part. How many of us have started out going to the gym religiously, only to stop after a few weeks or a few months?

With leadership behavior, maintaining change is even harder because you're altering your patterns of communication and interpersonal interaction. Thus, we strongly recommend hiring a coach, and sharing your development plan with your boss, selected peers, and your direct reports as well. The more public you are about the change you're trying to achieve, the more likely you are to stick to it. Furthermore, sharing your plan publicly, and then honoring your plan with integrity, is quite likely to improve the confidence that others have in you, and we all know how important that is!

# CHAPTER 5

## CREATING YOUR DEVELOPMENT PLAN

The LSI and 360 degree feedback are both excellent mechanisms for identifying patterns of strengths and weaknesses and creating a development plan. The LSI can be completed by one person (you) in 12-14 minutes and is most effective at predicting future success as a leader. The 360 requires the input of a number of raters and is therefore more time consuming and in need of a good deal of administrative work. It is most effective in pinpointing how your colleagues are experiencing your leadership in recent times. Whenever we coach executives or managers in development planning following the LSI or a 360-degree feedback assessment, we see the same pattern: people open their assessments, look for the areas where they are rated lowest, and start talking about ways to move those scores up. It's a real temptation: we all want to win, and we're conditioned to think that winning in the professional development arena means overcoming weaknesses first.

While it certainly can be important to overcome weaknesses, particularly if they are weaknesses in the Tragic Triangle competencies of Communicating the Vision, Fostering Teamwork, or Empowering the people around you, many of our clients have been surprised to learn that not all low scores are worth caring about, let alone working to improve.

Laying out your development plan is your opportunity to distinguish yourself from those around you. You do this by identifying key strengths and seeking ways to build on and highlight them. The essential point is this: spend your time and self-development resources wisely. They are, in a sense, scarce. Identify the competencies in which you have the chance to cross a major cusp, and consider putting real effort there. Identify also those areas that are most important to your role, and that you expect to be most important to future roles, and consider putting real effort there as well.

Remember also that people's experience of your leadership isn't isolated to a single behavior or cluster of behaviors. Instead, it's holistic, and studies (notably ours) show that leadership behaviors are tightly correlated. Changes in one behavioral dimension influence people's experience of you as a whole leader, a whole person, and that's why those changes show up not just in one area, but in your whole profile as a leader.

As we've discussed, behavior change is a hard road. Few people who set out to make lasting changes in their behavior truly succeed. We've identified and discussed the essential conditions that you must meet if you are to succeed in changing your leadership behavior – the crystallization of discontent, a focal event, and follow-up and follow-through – and creating your development plan is perhaps your best opportunity to ensure that these conditions are in place from the beginning. In our coaching practice, the creation of development plans is almost always a one-on-one exercise that we design as a focal event that will help point the way toward lasting behavior change.

Beyond the mechanics of lasting behavior change, we've also discussed the opportunities people find to make the changes that matter most: when you "cross the cusp" either to reach the top 20% of leaders in a given area, or to climb out of the bottom 10%, your change has a far greater impact than it would if you made incremental improvement "in the middle." Already, then, you have an indication of something to look for in plotting your development plan.

Without question you cannot begin a program of behavior change without knowing where to start and where you want to end up. This is why we opened this book with the self-assessment instrument that we hope you completed before you started reading. Now that you've taken the assessment and reviewed your results, you have a sense of where you stand on your leadership journey. Deciding where to go on that journey is up to you.

Self awareness – the quality of knowing where you stand, what your strengths, weaknesses, skills, talents, desires, hopes, and relationships are – is essential to your ability to grow and change in a conscious way. Opportunities to build self-awareness are everywhere, whether through formal assessments like the Leadership Success Indicator you took at the beginning of this book, or 360-degree feedback instruments, executive coaching, or other informed and expert-led conversation. Your own personal introspection can also lead you to expanding self-awareness, though of course the first step in powerful introspection is to uncover and understand your own filters or "blind spots," and this is no easy task. In fact, without outside intervention, you can't identify your own blind spots. That is, after all, why they're called "blind spots."

We strongly recommend using an executive coach to help you understand your assessment results and to begin plotting a course toward achieving your leadership potential.

As we've mentioned, most people open their assessment report and turn pages looking for their lowest scores immediately. Typically, they spend less time seeking to understand their strengths than they do trying to figure out why they're rated lower in other areas and what to do about that. It's possible to create a development plan that does nothing but address weaknesses, but as we've said it's not a good idea. The key to effective development planning lies in understanding what to work on, and how to tackle it.

### The Importance of Multiple Perspectives

Without question, you can use your LSI results alone to identify strengths and weaknesses and to form a development plan. That said, without the input of the people around you especially as you refine and progress through your plan, you're not likely to develop very far. We've pretty well hammered home the point that leadership arises in the experience of the followers. The Leadership Success Indicator is a useful tool in helping to uncover your philosophy of leadership. In that sense it can point toward your potential and your likely trajectory if you don't change, and it can give focus to areas where you should or must build skill. The LSI can also be deployed as a 360-degree feedback instrument to obtain the added benefit of multiple perspectives.

Certainly you can speak to the people around you, and ask them for candid feedback about your strengths and weaknesses. If you think, though, that your direct reports and other subordinates are going to be completely honest in telling you what they don't like about your leadership style, you are deluded. We know that you are a wonderful and magnanimous person with a deeper well of grace and equanimity than the Dalai Lama, but let's face facts: the people who report to you are afraid of you. You have power over their careers, their pay, and their security, and so they will never tell you the ugly truth about you (sorry... there is ugly truth about us too and our staff would never tell us about ours either) in person. It is the confidentiality and guaranteed anonymity of a well-formed 360-degree feedback process that largely frees people from fear of consequences and gives you a cleaner, clearer, deeper look into yourself.

### *Filter your assessment results*
### Confirmations & Surprises:

Start with an accounting of your assessment results. Grab a piece of paper and a pencil and make two columns on it. Label one "Self" and the other "all others." Starting in the "self" column, begin listing your strengths. List your strengths as you think they are, and then review your self-assessment to see if you've left anything out. Then, open your 360-degree feedback report and find the page that summarizes the top ten (or whatever number) highest- and lowest-rated items.

As we've said, virtually every time we have coached anyone with a 360-degree feedback assessment, the first thing they have done is to flip around looking for the page that has their highest- and lowest-rated items, and then laser in on the lowest. Right then, they typically start thinking of reasons why they might be rated low in that area, or circumstances that might have influenced people to rate them that way on that particular day.

Naturally, you're not going to do this, because you're more enlightened than all of those thousands of people we've coached. Right. Okay, set a timer and take the next two minutes and thirty seconds to stare at your weaknesses and wonder.

Good. Now that you're done with that, let's get back to work.

Using your full assessment report and your two-column sheet of paper, list your strengths as others see them. Make a mark next to anything that is a surprise – areas where others think you are strong, but where you may not. Circle all the "confirmations" where you and they agree.

Next, do the same exercise for your weaknesses. We'll repeat at this point that virtually every leadership development and HR group calls these things something like "opportunities" or "development areas," or some similarly euphemistic nonsense. That's fine, and of course you are welcome to call them what you like, but although it is far from politically correct, we favor straight talk in leadership development as in other things. We are all stronger in some things and weaker in others.

When you have completed these lists and marked areas of surprise and of confirmation, take a few moments to reflect on what you've seen. What themes are emerging? What do these similarities and differences of opinion and perspective reveal about you and your own level of self-awareness? If you've already gotten a bit uncomfortable and had a feeling like, "hmm, I didn't know that, and I didn't even know that I didn't know it," that's a clue that you're seeing into a blind spot. Write down a thought or two about what trait, attitude, or behavior might be inside that blind spot.

### Themes, obvious and otherwise:

Look again at that summary page of your LSI report. This time, look for themes. You might see that three or four of your highest-rated behaviors pertain to building relationships, or to client focus, or to driving for results, or something else. Make note of these themes – these are your consensus strengths. Do the same exercise for your weaknesses.

Some themes may not be particularly clear at first, and this is where an executive coach with strong skills and experience in working with various assessments including 360-degree feedback mechanisms can be particularly helpful. Having an additional perspective here to ask a few questions and help focus your reflection in this area is enormously helpful, perhaps even critical.

## What matters most?

Next, let's start looking at your job, and how your leadership behaviors, philosophy, and style influence your performance there. Make some notes about what is important in your role. What skills or attributes matter most? Without question, you're better off putting effort into development opportunities (whether these are enhancing strengths or improving in weak areas) that are most relevant to the job you're doing or the job you want to do.

While this often seems to go without saying, too often we see people focus so relentlessly on the areas where they have rated lowest that they overlook the items most relevant to their role. Again, the presence and input of an executive coach is helpful here to keep you on track and to help avoid these common and sometimes seemingly unavoidable pitfalls.

By now you should have a pretty good list going. You've identified some strengths and some weaknesses, and begun filtering these according to their relevance to your current or hoped-for role. Perhaps this has narrowed your list of potential development targets a bit. Next, let's apply another filter.

## Find chances to cross the cusps

Remember the concept of crossing the cusps? Here's your opportunity to put it into action. If you find yourself rated as challengedin any competency, it is obviously worth your most urgent consideration. If that competency is of high relevance to your work, then without question you must address the gap between your current and expected performance. Your career is quite likely in jeopardy otherwise.

Fortunately, most people don't find themselves in that position, and we'd submit that if you're intelligent and ambitious enough to be reading this book you are likely not in that unhappy place. That said if you are in that unhappy place, then at least part of your work in identifying development opportunities is done. In all probability you have also experienced the crystallization of discontent upon seeing your results, and while that may be painful, as we've seen it is a very good thing. Get to work.

No less important, you may find areas where you have an opportunity to cross the Exemplary cusp. That is, you may be able to move from say, the 75th to the 91st percentile, for example in a competency area. If that is the case, you have the chance to become the "go-to person" in your area, and thus potentially to take a significant step forward in your career. These are excellent targets of opportunity in a development plan.

### Focus on the critical few

Too often in our coaching practice we see highly earnest, profoundly ambitious people who believe that their path to Exemplary Leadership lies in being rated as exceptional in every competency – and who believe that they'll have to work on everything themselves to make that happen. No strength is too immaterial to live with as is, nor can any weakness be tolerated. When we ask them to write a development plan on their own, they come back with a 26-page document overburdened with lofty but unrealistic expectations and unreachable targets. Frequently, these targets are vague and ill-formed despite the bulk of their plans. Plainly said this is a prescription for failure if not disaster. Don't do this to yourself.

Instead, pick 3 development targets – two strengths to bulwark, and one weakness to improve. If you have two critical weaknesses to shore up – in other words, two areas where you must cross a "challenged" cusp to survive as a leader – then by all means, as we have said, put focus there. If you have a key strength opportunity that is highly relevant to your role, without question focus on it. Do not, however, overburden yourself. Remember the keys to effective change, and particularly remember the importance of follow-up and follow-through. Set yourself up for success by focusing on two or three achievable targets. Remember also the principle of the holistic experience of the leader – as you improve in one competency area, you will rise in others as well.

### Get specific, and keep it simple

Chances are that if you've worked in a corporate environment for more than, say, eleven minutes, you have encountered the term "SMART goals." We like this acronym when it's well-applied, and your development plan gives you the opportunity to apply it exceptionally well. For those who've not encountered it before, we use the SMART acronym this way: Specific, Measurable, Attainable, Realistic, and Time-bound. Let's add an "S" at this point for Simple. Setting an overly complex goal in the name of specificity does no one any good. In fact, it threatens to undermine the entire edifice of SMART goal planning and turn goals into the dreaded DUMB goal framework: Demeaning, Unworkable, Meaningless, and Bad. Nobody wants that.

So, now that you've done the analysis work, set a few goals. If you see that you have a strength in building relationships, for example, and a chance to become a world-class relationship builder, this would be a great area to set some SMART goals. An example goal statement might be "I will create 5 new, successful relationships with Vice-Presidents in Technology, Finance, Marketing, and HR by July. Success is receiving at least 3 unsolicited, incoming calls from each for consultation, appreciation, or invitation to a business function by that time." A goal like this sets an overall objective (new relationships) with specific identifiers (VPs in the various functions), as well as a specific success measure that is objective and quantifiable (number of unsolicited incoming calls), and a timeline (by July). It's also an attainable and realistic goal; a good relationship builder can certainly create 5 new relationships within a timeline. Making this number 50 would change things dramatically. The point is to do something that will challenge and stretch you, but that won't leave you feeling like you have to climb Mt. Everest, run a marathon, and swim the English Channel all on the same day.

### Get it under control

As you consider items for your development plan, ask yourself if the issue you're thinking of tackling is really yours. Is this a personal strength to highlight, or a personal weakness to overcome? You're a great deal more likely to succeed at changing what's under your control than trying to tackle a team or group problem. Identify the specific aspects of your behavior that underlie group concerns, and work on those. Define specific, measurable steps to lead toward success.

### Apply your understanding of the Golden Triangle

Remember that the six Golden Triangle competencies, three Magic and three Tragic, work together and influence one another. The secret of this is that you don't need to work directly on "Inspires Confidence," for example, to see improvements in how the people around you experience your ability to generate confidence in your leadership. The competencies are so highly correlated with one another that as you improve your abilities in some areas, you will almost without question improve in others as well.

This is especially true of building relationships, which as you'll recall is so highly correlated with driving for results that one nearly cannot happen without the other. While the remaining correlations are not quite as overwhelmingly strong, they are nonetheless incredibly powerful. Consider these when putting together your development plan. These correlations are clues to exemplary leadership.

We worked with a group of senior leaders in a Major Medical Center. Their teams, about 100 people in total, had for two years performance and morale issues. The Chief Administrator of the Hospital decided to use 360 feedback as a means of providing feedback to the key leadership of the hospital as well as providing them with their first leadership development opportunities. We put the director and two layers of management through a 360-degree feedback process. Each of the leaders worked with a coach to get a clear focus on their individual development opportunities. The same individuals then repeated the 360 about 18 months later. Each of the competencies represented in the chart below demonstrates a dramatic improvement in the rating averages over that time period. The leadership members focused on their development goals and maintained regular feedback as the year and a half progressed.

The results were dramatic and are summarized in the chart below. The important thing to note is that while the team showed the biggest change in the competency of "Innovation," *every single competency area showed improvement.* The chart illustrates our point for this chapter: leadership is holistic, and as people experience your improvement in one area, they will often experience improvements in others, too.

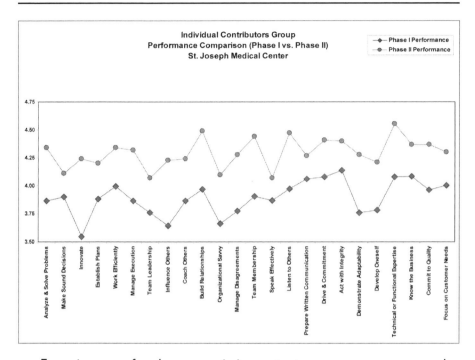

Focusing on a few key areas is important as you prepare your development plan. As we've said, first you must resist the temptation simply to dive into your weakest areas. In addition, though, you must also take a real accounting of yourself. It is tempting indeed to try to explain away, or deny our weaknesses. "Oh, I know Jim rated me really low in that area; he's just upset about x, y, or z." If you find yourself saying something like that, we hope you have the benefit of a coach who can probe more deeply into your statement. Remember what we said earlier: rationalization, denial, and justification are legitimate reactions. Don't confuse legitimate with useful.

Preparing and working through a development plan successfully is not an easy task and it's important to get plenty of input and lots of support. We strongly recommend having a coach work with you, one-on-one, to create your plan. As strongly as we recommend that step, we also encourage you to share your development plan with others. It's great to share it with your boss (this will provide plenty of motivation for the all-important follow-up and follow-through part of the change process) and great to share it with others at work, too.

Remember the story of John, the micromanaging executive we told you about in the previous chapter? John did something particularly brilliant when he shared his development plan: he asked three people he trusted and admired to get together with him monthly for six months to support him in achieving his development goals. The key in forming a team to keep you on track like this is to ensure that they see and understand the behaviors you are looking to change, and of course, to ensure that they will be absolutely candid with you. In John's case, it turned out beautifully. Consider creating a small, trusted circle like this to support you in achieving your development targets. We think you'll be pleased with the results.

| CRITICAL DEVELOPMENT PLANNING MISTAKES & SOLUTIONS | | |
|---|---|---|
| **Mistake** | **Description** | **What to Do** |
| Too many development objectives | It is not unusual for a leader to desire to be the best at everything. So they take on too many objectives. When this happens they often become overwhelmed with the commitment to complete them all. Consequence: often nothing is done. | 1. Remember: LSI competencies are correlated. Improving in one eventually spreads to improvement in others.<br>2. If the LSI shows Low Cusp Scores on any of the Magic Competencies, focus on these.<br>3. Limit development objectives to one or two that will have the greatest impact. |
| Incomplete Plan | A well constructed plan includes clear objectives, action steps to accomplish these, resources needed (including people who must support the plan), timing and measures. | 1. Once the objectives are selected, define these in terms of the outcome. What will be different<br>2. Identify the steps necessary to accomplish these.<br>3. Attach dates for step completion<br>4. Include measures: these can vary: %, $, Quality, Quantity, Action Completed |
| Execution/Follow-up is missing | Once started, people will often stop executing. This happens because they do not think about a follow-up and feedback strategy. | 1. Include a follow-up or feedback action step for each objective<br>2. Establish a small group of trusted people to provide continuous feedback to you on your progress. This will be two or three people who have the skills you are trying to develop, who will be able to observe you and who agree to provide you feedback ad hoc and on a regular basis. |

| | | |
|---|---|---|
| Action Steps are not Specific or out of sequence | Too often the objective is clear but the action steps remain too broad. They often encompass two or three steps. They may be out of sequence. | 1. Break down each objective into discrete steps. An action should be one imperative sentence and include a clear verb & objective. (i.e., review budget plan by 2/1/08. Call George to review plan by 2/6/2008. Draft final plan by 2/9/08. <br> 2. Review the steps to make sure that they fall into a logical sequence. Change the sequence as necessary. <br> 3. Get as detailed as you can about these steps. |
| Feedback on the Plan is not sought or accepted | Often leaders shy away from showing their development plan to others. They might be concerned about showing weakness. The real truth is this shows strength. Anyone with enough character to demonstrate they are committed to improving leadership skills becomes a role model for others. Showing the plan and asking for feedback is critical to keeping commitments to others. It builds trust | 1. Start showing the plan to boss, direct reports, peers and others who might be affected by the changes in your behavior. <br> 2. Accept their feedback. Incorporate their ideas into your action steps. <br> 3. Present the revised plan to them. <br> 4. Agree with them on timely reviews of progress. (quarterly, monthly) |

# CHAPTER 6

# THE DIRTY LITTLE SECRET THAT YOU SHOULD KNOW ABOUT CORPORATE LEADERSHIP DEVELOPMENT PROGRAMS

Robert, a 22-year veteran of one of America's most recognizable man-ufacturing companies, responded with an emphatic "yes" to the beau-tifully-embossed, hand-signed invitation of the CEO to join a group of highly-respected, long-tenured executives at a 3-day Leadership Devel-opment conference. To begin, Robert thought, you really don't say no to the CEO. Beyond that, the conference sounded like a really great time – a chance to catch up with people he hadn't seen in months, a chance to unwind, play a little golf, relax, and enjoy a few nights on the company's tab at the Four Seasons. Not too bad a trade for sitting in a room for a few hours listening to a couple speakers and filling out a couple forms that HR is asking for. Not too bad at all…

About two weeks later, an emerging leader on Robert's staff had a somewhat different experience: Lauren was unpacking boxes as she moved into her new, larger cubicle, having been promoted a week prior to her first middle management position. Now, rather than managing one team of five graphic designers, she was responsible for leading a team of thirty-five, with five direct reports. In turn, each of Lauren's direct reports managed between 3 and 9 designers spread out over two continents. Lauren now had staff in no fewer than five time zones. Gulping as she prepared for her first staff meeting, Lauren reached out for a couple of her favorite books on leadership and her notes from the "introduction to management" course that she downloaded from the company's intranet.

Next, Lauren picked up the phone and dialed Robert's office, hop-ing she could grab him for a few minutes for a little last-minute advice. She liked and admired Robert; he was pleasant, kind, and most of all, available when she had questions. Lauren had confidence in Robert's ability to lead, and relied on him as something of a mentor. She knew that Robert had been instrumental in her promotion and she was proud of being seen as a rising star in the design shop.

That day, however, Robert wasn't available.    In fact at the time Lauren called his office hoping for a few words of wisdom, Robert was somewhere on the back nine, enjoying the heck out of his Leadership Development conference.

Of course, Lauren was fine and she has done well in her role, and there was nothing at all wrong with Robert accepting the CEO's invitation.    Robert (now retired) was a hard-working man who earned his success, to be sure.   There is a point, though, and it's pretty simple:

### Most companies have leadership development fundamentally backwards.

Here's why: across Corporate America, the vast majority of funds allocated to leadership development are spent on the most senior leaders.   Ironically, these are the leaders who benefit the least from development.  They change the least, they grow the least, and although they are responsible often for huge organizations that contribute substantially to the bottom line, the dollars spent on their development likely have far less impact than desired if the measure is something like "growth in profit" or "increased productivity," or if one were to measure changes in their 360-degree feedback scores over time.

We're convinced that one reason why the departments responsible for leadership development struggle so mightily to prove the return on their investments is because they're investing their money and other resources on efforts that don't promise much return at all.   In our opinion, these groups should stop looking for returns in performance or profitability from these programs and should present them as relationship-building opportunities for senior leaders.   There is real and important value in senior leaders building and growing these relationships; let's acknowledge that and move on.

The longer someone has been in a leadership position, the less their assessment results change in response to any single intervention or input.  This isn't about assessment results, though – it's about people actually changing. Remember the three fundamental conditions that must be in place for people to change: the crystallization of discontent, a focal event, and follow-up and follow through. Now, imagine how difficult it is to achieve those three conditions with a leader who has achieved the pinnacle of career success.

Don't get us wrong: we think that the majority of senior leaders in organizations are in their roles for good reason. They contribute at an extremely high level. The best of them are truly exceptional leaders.

Conversely, newer leaders, leaders like Lauren, change and develop a great deal. This simply makes intuitive sense: think about how young people grow and develop. New leaders, while they may or may not be chronologically young, are "young" in terms of their experience arc. Good ones – the ones we all hope will grow to become senior leaders – seek out and use information that helps them grow, build, and tune their leadership skills. Moreover they apply it, seek more of it, apply that, and soon they are in the midst of a virtuous circle of growth and development.

We've seen the same pattern in nearly every large corporation we've visited. Programs for the most senior leaders are often huge-budget affairs with loads of amenities, lovely catering, and high-ticket speakers flogging their books. We're delighted to be included in some of them and we flog the heck out of our book, too. Yet we're keenly aware that the real development work belongs to the junior and middle managers, and the fresher senior managers, who are actually confronting the gap between who they are today and who they need to be as leaders to be as successful as they'd like.

In today's business environment, few companies are spending lavishly on anything. Still, they focus the great majority of their leadership development dollars on the top of the house, as it were. Meanwhile, managers deeper down in the hierarchy are increasingly left to their own devices as programs are scaled back or cancelled outright.

We have a simple argument to make: if you want to boost the return on the money you're investing in leadership development, spend more money and time on less-senior leaders.

75

## Danger and Opportunity

To us it seems that the traditional, top-down approach to leadership development is a little like building a pyramid upside down. A great deal of effort has to go in to balancing the pyramid and keeping it supported, and eventually, no matter what you do the pyramid will fall over on its side. The danger, of course, is that organizations that take this top-down approach will ultimately fail to develop a sufficient base of effective, high-functioning leaders to fill their senior-most roles with the best leaders.

Succession planning in many organizations reflects this danger. It's still often a vertical, hierarchically-based, and stovepipe effort that pulls the current leader's favored subordinates toward the top, too often irrespective of their actual leadership ability. When those chosen few arrive at the top of the food chain, they might be great leaders or they might be just terrible. They'll likely be invited to participate in some leadership development programs, but by then it will typically be too late for many of them.

Moreover, many of these leaders reach these positions after long periods, or even whole careers, in the same division or silo of an organization. Thus their ability to take on the role of general manager is hampered. Many of these people may have outstanding relationships within their silos, but far fewer across multiple functions or channels, let alone the whole value chain. To inspire confidence, build an outstanding network of highly connected relationships, and drive effectively for results, we argue that senior leaders must have greater exposure to the breadth of leadership skills as well as depth in their business discipline or functional expertise.

The opportunity is for individuals to turn this trend around, not just by seeking out opportunities to drive leadership development programs deeper into the organization, but also by developing yourself. Obviously you've taken one such step by buying and reading this book. We hope you've taken the self-assessment we provided in the preface, and used the results and some of our development planning tools to build your development plan, too.

Another opportunity is to gather with like-minded people and create your own leadership development program, formal or otherwise. No one ever said you had to have permission to start a conversation, after all, and that's exactly what leadership development is, at its heart: a conversation between you and the people around you, seeking to improve their experience of you as a leader.

Remember the keys as you engage in the conversation: inspire confidence, build relationships, and drive for results. Communicate the vision, foster teamwork, empower others. Remember also that improving in one area almost results in your improving in others, too.

Your leadership development conversation can go in almost any direction and include almost anyone you wish to include, thanks to the tools and resources available on the web. This underscores our point about the opportunity as well as the danger inherent in so many organizations' approach to leadership development. The costs of leadership development are dropping – many tools, frankly, are available for free. Obviously people's time is valuable, and the knowledge gathered by a dedicated team of leadership development experts inside a company can be genuinely invaluable, especially if it's well-applied through good decision-making.

Our challenge to you, irrespective of where you are in the organizational hierarchy, is to start a conversation about leadership development. You might start by sharing your own development plan with your manager, your direct reports, and some peers. You might visit with your HR partner or other senior managers and inquire about the structure of your organization's leadership development programs. Ask about what's planned for new managers, and help shape how they are supported.

The higher you rise in the organization, the more valuable your time becomes, especially if you become a mentor to others. You may have, or have had, a mentor yourself. If so, we have almost no question that you remember how valuable her advice and counsel was. Many people who have had a good mentor want to give that gift to others, too. We hope you do. Consider that there's a selfish reason to mentor others, too: your leadership effectiveness increases with each mentoring experience you take on. Remember the importance of building relationships, empowering others, fostering teamwork, and of course, inspiring confidence. Effective mentors do all these things simultaneously, and they do them in ways that provide lasting, memorable value for the people they touch.

The world of leadership development does, at times, seem to be somewhat upside down. It's true that the people who need it least (or at least, benefit the least) tend to get the most resources in leadership development. That said, there is great opportunity out there across organizations as well as around the world. We encourage you to work toward allocating your company's leadership development time and money more sensibly. We also encourage you to take matters into your own hands, as it were, and create your own leadership development conversation.

# CHAPTER 7

## SELECTING AND DEVELOPING THE LEADERS AROUND YOU

When Jack Welch became CEO at General Electric, he began looking for and grooming his successors. He started by identifying a number of people he felt had the potential to lead GE, and he invested time, energy, and effort in their development. Welch understood intuitively that the great leaders don't just lead teams in the here and now; they also focus time and attention on shaping the future of the organization. They identify, select, develop, and even nurture other leaders.

There's nothing new about the notion that learning and development arise in a cycle in which one learns, builds skill, and finally attains mastery through teaching that skill or "giving it away," to borrow a phrase. The model of the guilds of craftsmen still works: one apprentices under the guidance of a master, becomes a journeyman skilled enough to produce fine work on his or her own, and finally, one masters his or her craft and then takes apprentices, training them so that they can carry on the craft's traditions and ultimately expand the craft.

The best leaders choose to "give it away" and help those around them grow their own leadership skill. They understand the strategic value of developing others. More importantly, they seek out the best ways to do this.

Developing those around you speaks directly to the competency of "Empowers." The connection here is clear: in providing opportunities to those around you to stretch, to grow, and to face challenges that will hone their skills for the future, you're expanding their power and influence. Clearly, then, there's a payoff in terms of your own leadership value.

Beyond the selfish reasons for helping others to grow (and make no mistake – we're firmly in favor of acting in your enlightened self-interest), leaders who help others to develop provide enormous value to their organizations. These leaders stand at the intersection of their organization's present success and its future demands. They have knowledge of the skills that will be required in the future organization, and they can provide the best current answer to the question of whether to "build" leadership talent from within or whether to "buy" that talent on the outside market.

Given the costs inherent in recruiting, on-boarding, and developing newly-hired executives, both in terms of the financial outlay for recruiting, salary, and relocation costs and in terms of the time-to-productivity cost, the answer to that "build versus buy" question in many firms is biased toward build. Yet many organizations don't do this nearly as well as they would like.

If you position yourself as one of the chief builders of talent, not only are you serving your organization what it needs, you are also building an unshakable reputation and a network of strong relationships across the organization. Remember the importance of the "Builds Relationships" competency as you think about helping those around you to develop and grow their leadership skill. In particular, remember that of the Magic Triangle competencies, "Builds Relationships" is so tightly correlated with "Drives for Results" that our research suggests that the two practically rise and fall together: strong relationships, strong results. Weak relationships, weak results. No relationships... well, you get the idea.

So the case for developing others is pretty straightforward: help yourself, help your organization, and help others. You can prioritize those in any order that you like, and the case is equally strong. The real question is, "how do you do it?"

The truth is that there are a lot of people and organizations involved in leadership development. Inside large companies there are usually groups, typically within HR, which carry leadership development as their charter. Smaller companies may do this less formally or with fewer people, but ordinarily it's still an endeavor that has at least some of the chief executives' attention.

Some people see the existence of a leadership development team as a good reason not to think much about helping those around them to grow and develop their skills. "We'll let HR take care of that," they think, and each year they dutifully check off the boxes of completing performance evaluations, nominating someone from their team to attend a leadership development program, and perhaps filling out a 360-degree feedback form for one or two people. Their work is done, right?

Wrong. The best leaders understand that the leadership development group can't do much more than make opportunities available, provide some (we hope) powerfully useful tools, and facilitate some conversations. The real work of leadership development happens on the ground. It happens between emerging leaders and the people around them. It happens in conversations between established leaders and newly-minted supervisors. Development happens as a function of people solving increasingly difficult problems.

Importantly, development work happens between senior leaders and the people they mentor. The true emerging leadership talent isn't necessarily the guy who's at the office until 11pm every night. It's the person turning up in the Senior Vice President's office looking for opportunities to stretch, grow, and learn. Senior leaders who have good instincts or solid leadership skills seek out people like this and groom them with mentorship, challenge, and opportunities. It is in these relationships – in observing how great leaders work and in working under their stewardship – that emerging leaders truly learn the craft. Development programs and book learning can provide an important foundation but nothing can replace the actual practice of craft.

Author Dave was a clinical psychologist and spent many years in school learning the discipline. Leaving aside the easy jokes about learning discipline in the first place (really... we're leaving them aside and it's not easy for us to do that), Dave emerged from school with a freshly-minted Ph.D degree and felt ready to tackle the world of psychotherapy. During his first several months Dave worked with a senior psychologist. In the first several weeks of this practical introduction to the craft, Dave learned more about the actual practice of psychology than he did during his entire academic career. Seeing how it was done in practice, and then having the chance to debrief, inquire, and debate, drove learning far faster and deeper. All of Dave's academic preparation was critically important of course, but it was the practical application that brought it into focus.

The same is typically true for leaders in organizations: the real learning comes through experience, reflection, and feedback with masters of the craft. To become a master, you must travel not only the path of the apprentice and journeyman, but you must also take on apprentices of your own.

HR and a Leadership Development group can help create the context and provide the tools and processes that will help people along their path. If your organization has a Strategic Planning function, it would be great if HR and Strategic Planning worked together to forecast the portfolio of skills that the organization will require to fulfill on its mission. Whether they do so or not, it is really up to the people in line management functions, and the individual contributors in the field, to do the actual development work.

### Developing Others: Create a Baseline
If someone blindfolded you and flew you around for several hours, and then gave you the keys to a new car and said, "drive this to San Francisco," chances are one of the first things you'd want to know is where you are right now. After all, the route to San Francisco is pretty different if you're starting in Seattle than if you're starting in Phoenix. And if you head off to the South when you ought to be going North, driving faster is only going to make things worse.

The same is true for leadership development: it's important to know where you're starting from, and where you're going to. In today's organizations, it's rare to find anyone who has time to wander around exploring and hoping to find the finish line.

First, be sure you understand your own philosophy of leadership. We hope that, having read this book, you'll understand our research, its scientific value, and the point of view that comes from it: the truly great leaders focus on others, as well as themselves. They understand that leadership only arises in the experience of those around the leader. They know that inspiring confidence is critical to effective leadership. They don't just grasp the value of building relationships; they are active, effective, powerful relationship builders. And of course they keep a strong and reliable focus on getting results.

Does this match your philosophy of leadership? By now you've had the opportunity to look at yourself in the mirror, and to take an accounting of your strengths and weaknesses in relation to this model or philosophy of leadership. Now, you can begin to help others see into that mirror as well.

The thing is, first you need that mirror. A quick way to get a good insight into people's philosophy of leadership, and into their likely strengths and possible weaknesses, is to have them complete a self-assessment instrument like the LSI that you took at the beginning of this book. As a purchaser of the book you are entitled to take the LSI for free, and as we've repeated, we hope you have done so and used your results to your advantage. We invite you to contact us to discuss having the people around you take the LSI as well.

Remember that the LSI instrument reveals likely trajectory, and paints a picture of the subject's philosophy of leadership. This is why it's useful not only in selection (which we'll get to in a moment) but also in development. LSI results that show significant gaps in the "Magic Triangle" competencies of Inspires Confidence, Builds Relationships, and Drives for Results don't mean that the subject won't ever become a great leader. Similarly, LSI results that show weaknesses in the "Tragic Triangle" competencies of Communicates the Vision, Empowers, and Fosters Teamwork don't mean the end of the road, either. Instead, these are signals of opportunity, and keys to understanding how the person in question views leadership.

Properly interpreted, the LSI results will give the person in question a great place to start a conversation about what skills to develop, what traits to watch out for, and what steps she might take to increase her likelihood of becoming an exemplary leader. These results, though, really are a place to start. It's important to have more points of view – specifically, the input of her boss, direct reports, and peers – and then, of course, the opportunity to build skill and experience through real-life assignments and interactions.

### Developing others: 360-degree feedback

While 360-degree feedback is a widely accepted and at this point, well-known process, there's still some controversy about *how* to use it. Many organizations use 360-degree feedback for development purposes only. Others use it for performance evaluation and as a key input into decision-making about things like reassignment and promotion. Still other organizations take a blended approach.

In our experience the best use of 360 is development-only. When it's used this way, the results gathered in the assessment itself remain assuredly confidential. Knowing that the results themselves will never be known to anyone but the subject and a (hopefully external) coach, and knowing further that the subject will never know who gave which specific rating or made which specific comment (except for the boss, who is known since there is only one person in that category), frees people to be thoroughly candid. We strongly recommend that organizations bring in external coaches to help interpret 360-degree feedback results for the same reason: candor. Imagine a highly stressed leader looking at results that he thinks are going to prevent him from getting the prized assignment or promotion he wants – and trying to discuss a development plan with someone from the same company's HR department. Our experience shows that the leader in question simply will not engage in a coaching session with an internal coach – there is too much to protect and unfortunately, typically too few reasons to trust the process absolutely.

About 20 years ago with one of our first 360-degree feedback clients, we had a big scare when someone came to us and said, "something's really wrong with your scoring. I just had my performance review and my boss gave me stellar ratings. And your assessment shows my boss rating me really low here, here, and here. This just can't be right!"

You can imagine that we were a little frenzied – this was literally our first client to adopt this tool, which was pretty new globally at the time. We wanted to be sure we had the utmost credibility. So we went to the boss to find out what happened. He told us right away, "There's nothing at all wrong with your scoring. I did give Bob a stellar performance review; I think Bob is generally a great guy and I didn't want to impact his potential raise or his career with a bad review. But since this feedback was going to stay just between me and him, I felt I could be really honest – and the truth is Bob needs to work on these things if he's going to lead at a higher level."

When this happened again, we were a bit surprised. The third time, we thought it just couldn't possibly be a coincidence. By the time we reached the end of our first year providing 360-degree feedback and coaching, we knew to anticipate this frantic inquiry, because nearly everyone we worked with had the same experience.

This is exactly the kind of candor we want to get from feedback. And we argue that it is only possible with total confidentiality, an external coach, and the knowledge that results are not going to be shared except with the express permission of the subject of the assessment.

While we feel that results should always stay confidential, we feel equally strongly that development plans should be shared with bosses, direct reports, and select peers. Naturally this should always be voluntary in order to promote candor among other positive traits. Sharing development plans builds on all six of the essential Golden Triangle competencies. Think about it: it communicates a vision by showing where a leader wants to go to work on his leadership. It fosters teamwork by getting others involved: "I'm really looking to improve my strategic thinking skills; I'd like to bounce a few ideas off of you, or meet with your team a few times a month to learn from you." It empowers others by giving them the opportunity to keep you accountable to your own development plan.

Think now of the other three Golden Triangle competencies, and how sharing one's development plan can improve how a leader is viewed in these areas. By achieving development goals, one inspires confidence in his ability to deliver. Perhaps more importantly, getting others involved in development activity builds relationships. Organizational life rarely promotes the kind of intimacy – the sharing of information that is important, personal, and gives others a view into one's vulnerabilities – the way that sharing a development plan does. This intimacy is the real glue of durable relationships. Lastly, as we have seen throughout the book, building relationships enhances a leader's ability to deliver results better than anything else.

In many of the organizations we've worked with, emerging and other leaders have formed "accountability teams" or "coaching circles" to promote their focus on development. These groups have worked exceptionally well in a number of cases: typically they consist of people from multiple disciplines, and because they exist outside of formal reporting relationships we have found them to be groups where candid and open dialogue thrives. Consider starting or fostering groups like this in your organization.

As you think about developing the emerging leaders around you, think about this: having them share development plans in a thoughtful way, but perhaps just a bit more broadly than they might do in their comfort zone, may be the single most powerful step that you and they can take together to start the development process.

This has implications for you, too, doesn't it? When is the last time you had a really candid conversation with a trusted colleague or a direct report about the areas in which you want to improve your own leadership? When is the last time you made a real, committed effort to expand that circle of trust? How would building a broader base of strong and trusting relationships impact your own leadership and your ability to help more people around you build their leadership skill?

Stop here and make a list of ten people you will reach out to over the next ten days. Pick five you'll take an interest in helping to grow, and five others you'll share your own development plans with. Get a little bit outside your comfort zone here. Stretch yourself to build others, to build relationships, foster teamwork, empower others, and inspire confidence.

### From Individual to Organizational: Key Factors in Developing Leaders

There are important leadership development functions that take place one-to-one or in very small groups – for example, self assessments, 360-degree feedback and the interpretation of results, creating individual development plans, and of course, doing the actual work to build skill.

All of this work, though, takes place inside an organization. The organization creates the context in which the development work takes place. Our research has shown clearly that there is an essentially universal contextfor exemplary leadership – the six Golden Triangle competencies that we've discussed throughout the book. Exemplary leaders, as we've seen, excel in the three Magic Triangle competencies of Inspires Confidence, Builds Relationships, and Drives for Results, and they do so because they have mastered the three Tragic Triangle competencies of Communicates the Vision, Fosters Teamwork, and Empowers.

Every organization, of course, has its own unique characteristics and its own culture. And many organizations have created or adopted leadership models that attempt to break their cultures and values down into a measurable set of behaviors. Your organization may well be one such place, and if you work for a large corporation this is even more likely. As you look to develop the people around you, look first at your organization's leadership model. How well does it reflect the six Golden Triangle competencies? Are all six in the model? They don't necessarily need to be worded precisely the way we've worded them in order to be present, but if one or more is simply not present, your organization's model needs a tune-up.

Look also at how well your organization's model reflects what is truly important inside the organization. We have often been surprised to discover that our clients have simply adopted a ready-made competency model simply because it was easy, or the consultants that have come before had ready-made 360-degree feedback instruments built on a model of their own. Leadership is both a global and a local phenomenon, and to be effective in an organization, a leader must "fit." Look again at your organization's leadership model and be sure it truly reflects the values and important characteristics of the company.

Use your influence and your knowledge to help your organization fine-tune its leadership model. Better still; consider putting together a group of people to partner with senior executives and HR to evolve the model. This will be a development opportunity for you and them as you foster teamwork between individuals and groups and as you build relationships that will pay off strongly in the future.

### Some very brief comments on Succession Planning

Many organizations, particularly large companies, spend at least some time on succession planning. Done well, succession planning processes consistently produce leaders who are better-qualified to run substantial portions of the organization than they would be otherwise. Effective succession planning helps organizations to decide whether to "build" from within or "buy" talent on the outside market. As we said earlier, effective succession planning reduces hiring and development costs, increases retention of high-value talent, and gives the organization a high-quality view of its talent portfolio.

We are consistently amazed at how many organizations have extraordinarily accurate inventories of equipment, supplies, and facilities, but almost no clue about what skills, talents, and aspirations their people have. Many of these companies profess that "people are our most important asset," and yet they treat these people with a great deal less care than they do their computers, telephones, or manufacturing equipment.

Granted, it's a great deal easier and more straightforward to repair a machine than it is to develop a person's leadership skill. Furthermore, the return on investment in machinery and processes is much easier to calculate because there are fewer variables. When it comes to developing people, the variables are endless and the potential outcomes, both positive and negative, are difficult to predict with precision. Nevertheless, effective succession planning gives organizations – both large and small – a great advantage in managing this most important resource of the human capital that makes it run.

So, how best to do it? The simple answer is to design and follow a succession planning system that builds and reinforces the six Golden

Triangle competencies. To begin, an organization must declare a vision for succession management; otherwise it may be better to do nothing at all. Clarity of vision, and a vision that is understood throughout the organization, gives everyone in the organization the opportunity to participate in some way, even if that participation is limited to understanding what the organization is doing and why.

Succession planning works best when it is designed to broaden the base of input into the selection, development, and placement of leaders being groomed for more senior roles. Organizations that routinely hold broad-based talent review sessions in which multiple people discuss the development and potential of a significant number of candidates work best. The best organizations hold these talent review sessions frequently – at least twice a year – and they are sponsored and led by the CEO. CEO leadership is essential if the system is to work across, between, and deep into the organization.

Returning to the Golden Triangle, methods that start with senior leader input and include broad constituencies inspire confidence, build relationships, and foster teamwork. An example might be a diversified financial services company at which talent review sessions include line of business leaders presenting talent profiles of people two- or even three-deep in their organizations to a panel of the CEO and all her direct reports. This gives people from multiple lines of business the opportunity to understand and provide input into emerging leaders, and more importantly the opportunity to help select them for new assignments that will build their breadth of leadership experience as well as line of business depth.

Our experience also shows that organizations that routinely move emerging leaders into new, breadth-developing assignments tend to have the strongest succession management results. In these organizations, emerging leaders work in multiple lines of business and become stronger general managers because they understand the strategic perspective more deeply. They understand and learn how to balance the competing demands of, for example, technology, marketing, product development, finance, and distribution. While this process may take many years, organizations that invest in a leader's development by facilitating her moves to multiple business units profit from having a broad base of leaders with outstanding relationships and the ability to foster teamwork within and between groups.

Other organizations are not so lucky. They approach succession planning with a siloed, top-down, vertical-only approach that promotes technology leaders only inside the technology group, or manufacturing leaders only within manufacturing, and so forth. The leaders who emerge from these systems are lucky indeed if they can foster teamwork effectively across and sometimes even within groups. Since fostering teamwork is one of the Tragic Triangle competencies, as we have seen, those who are unable to do these well can never achieve leadership greatness.

The implication of this for you as an individual leader should be clear: to build your own leadership strength you need to get involved in your organization's approach to succession planning. Perhaps more importantly, you need to become known in your organization as a "source of leadership talent." That means helping the best and brightest emerging leaders around you to take on new assignments outside of your group.

This is a challenging, sometimes painful, and seemingly counterintuitive thing to do: most people by nature want to hoard the talent around them. "Jane's my best regional sales manager. I couldn't possibly give her to the marketing group!" The truth is, when you do hoard talent, you're actually shortchanging yourself as well as your organization.

"Giving" Jane to the marketing group means that Jane has the opportunity first to help one of her more junior sales managers become just as great as she has been in that role. Moreover it means Jane has an opportunity to grow and develop new skills that will prepare her for even larger roles in the organization further on. Most importantly and most directly for you, helping Jane to take a new role in a different part of your organization gives you a trusted, strong relationship in that department or division (imagine Jane's gratitude knowing that you helped her get the role she wanted, even though it cost you her direct service in the short-term). You're building stronger relationships. You're fostering teamwork by sourcing and sharing talent. You're even further on your way to becoming an exemplary leader.

90

# BACKGROUND AND REVIEW OF THE LITERATURE

The research in the field of leadership would indicate that there are measures of personality strengths and shortcomings to predict future leadership success with relative accuracy (Bass, 1990; Howard and Bray, 1990; Hughes et al., 1993; Sorcher, 1985; Yukl, 1989). Yet DeVries (1992) has found that the failure rate for senior executives in the United States is over 50%. Judge (2002) noted that personality traits can predict leadership success with some accuracy. In recent years personality researchers have found that all personality traits and descriptions can be subsumed and completely explained by five general categories of personality traits. These five traits have become known as the Big Five. They are Extraversion, Conscientiousness, Openness, Agreeableness and Neuroticism. Of the so called Big Five personality traits, Extraversion, Conscientiousness, and Openness to experience all had a significant positive correlation with leadership success. Neuroticism had a significant negative correlation with leadership success and the fifth factor Agreeableness was not significantly related to leadership success. Judge states that we have no underlying theory of leadership that describes why such traits are related to leadership success.

The 50% leader failure rate produces enormous loses of revenue and forward movement on the part of institutions who must regularly replace their senior leaders. In addition to the revenue losses there often is a lapse of one year before a new candidate for the position is located, hired, oriented and begins to fully contribute.

The main reasons for this discrepancy between the state of the art and the state of the practice seem to be two pronged. First, psychologists who produce the findings of ways and means to successfully predict leadership success write primarily in obscure journals for other psychologists rather than for the business community. Second, corporations may chose not to utilize even those instruments that they know of for reasons of time, cost, fear of lawsuits or other business considerations.

Foushee, Chidester, Helmreich, et.al. studied the personality traits that impact team performance (Chidester, et. al., 1991; Foushee & Helmreich, 1988). It has been established that a lack of team cohesion and performance are the central causes of airline accidents (Cooper, White, & Lauber, 1979). Chidester, et. al. found that severity of errors is correlated with the Captains personality traits as manifested under pressure. Captains who were friendly and self-confident made the fewest errors. Captains who were arrogant and dictatorial made the most errors. Somewhat surprisingly personality is not measured in Pilot selection (Chidester, et. al., 1991).

The present research attempts to scientifically identify leaders bound for success or failure. Also the findings will be written in popular book form so that they are available to senior executives and Human Resources professionals.

Historically, leadership impact in the corporate world has been measured by business results. Most typically recent (last quarter or last year) results. Recent studies have indicated that the leadership ratings by colleagues-the consumers of leadership behavior-are more predictive of long-term leadership success (Bass, 1990; D. P Campbell, 1991; Harris & Hogan, 1992; Hughes, Ginnett, and Curphy, 1993; Yukl, 1989; Shipper and Wilson, 1999).

This accuracy appears to be due to the ability of colleagues to correct for business and product conditions. A leader who was the General Manager of cell phones when they first hit the market would likely have had great short-term financial success irrespective of their leadership skills. Contrariwise, a great leader put in charge of a difficult turn around or taking over a company or product that had been on hard times might be an exemplary leader but have negative short term results.

It should be clear that these accurate ratings are those given by colleagues, particularly Direct Reports. Self-ratings are poor predictors of leadership success (Farh & Dobbins, 1989). The exception is that consistent over-evaluation of one's own performance is a precursor of leadership failure (Atwater & Yammarino, 1992; Nilsen and Campbell, 1993; Van Velsor, Taylor & Leslie, 1992).

The authors have nearly 20,000 Multi-Rater or 360 Feedback results from executives in a variety of companies in about 20 countries covering North America, Europe and Asia. The typical Multi-Rater instrument measures a variety of competencies (e.g. Drives for Results, Builds Relationships, and Thinks Strategically). Each competency is measured by a group of items that purport to measure positive practices in the competency area.

Examples of such items would be:

> ➢ Takes responsibility for commitments and actions.
> ➢ Possesses high internal work standards.
> ➢ Sets ambitious yet attainable goals.
> ➢ Unhesitatingly makes decisions as required.
> ➢ Treats others with respect and fairness.
> ➢ Develops positive work relationships with all levels of the organization.

### Design of the study
The study at hand uses leaders from three US institutions. Silverthorne (2001) did cross cultural research using the Big Five to examine whether those traits would be predictive of leadership effectiveness. The study used executives from the U.S., China and Thailand. The most discrepant findings were those of the U.S and Thailand. In this study the effective managers from the U.S. scored higher on extraversion, agreeableness, conscientiousness, and openness. They scored lower on Neuroticism. In Thailand only Extraversion (higher scores) and Neuroticism (lower scores) differentiated the two groups.

Our research has found similar cultural differences in which competencies related to leadership success. Therefore, this study was limited to U.S. institutions. The findings cannot be generalized to other cultures and their leaders.

The companies used in this study are a major communications company, a chain of hospitals and the Public Health Department of a major city. The subjects constitute a subsection of all the Multi Rater instruments in our database.

Each leader was graded by taking the average score achieved on all items (typically about 70) from all other raters. This did not include the subject's self-rating. In this study Subjects were rated by their Manager, their Peer group and their Direct Report group. The top ten percent were designated Exemplary Leaders (EL) and the lowest ten percent were designated as Failed Leaders (FL). The average scores of the two groups are displayed in Figure A. The scores on each of the nineteen competencies were significantly different at the $p<.01$ level or greater. Stated differently the ELs were rated far higher than the FLs on every measure. Two very different groups were identified.

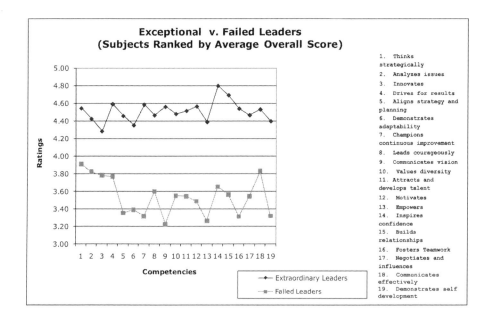

A number of the subjects took the same Multi-Rater instrument 18 months after their first administration. This allowed measures of improvement against stated objectives. Peterson, 1993; Peterson and

Hicks (1993) found that most managers positively changed their targeted behaviors and found these changes holding six months later.

There were five research hypotheses:
1. That the EL group would rate themselves higher than the FL group but by a significantly smaller margin than did their colleagues.
2. That there would be a consistently different self response profile between the EL and FL groups.
3. That the items, if any, on which the two groups self-ratings significantly differed could be successfully used as a stand alone self-scoring instrument to measure the extent to which a new subjects profile matched that of the two Leader groups.
4. That the test-retest group would show significant improvement on their targeted goals over an 18 month period.
5. That FLs would significantly overrate themselves compared to the ratings of Others.

### Research Results
1. The first hypothesis was confirmed. The EL group average self-rating was 4.15. The FL group average self-rating was 3.99. The difference is not significant. So colleagues rate the two groups more differently than they rate themselves. Interestingly the FL group rate themselves higher than the EL group on 12% of the items.
2. The second hypothesis was confirmed. There was a consistently different response pattern between the members of the two groups. In fact, 58 items were found on which the two groups self scores differed significantly.
3. These items have been used to formulate a Leadership Inventory Scale (LIS) to be used as a freestanding self-rating instrument. One goal of this research is that this instrument will demonstrate sufficient validity and reliability to be gainfully used as a part of a successful hiring, promotion, high potential identification processes.

The items which produced significantly different results were as follows:

Items where the EL group rated themselves significantly higher than the FL group.
1. Is approachable.
2. Develops effective working relationships with higher management.
3. Builds collaborative 5relationships outside functional area.
4. Actively forms partnerships with external organizations working in the same or related areas.
5. Maintains effective working relationship with peers.
6. Maintains effective working relationships with peers.
7. Arrives at meetings on time.
8. Champions positive change in the organization.
9. Continually improves customer service skills within the work unit.
10. Adjusts priorities according to changing organizational needs.
11. Prepares people to understand the reason for change.
12. Conveys a sense of mission that inspires motivates others.
13. Communicates clearly about the future direction of the organization.
14. Presents ideas clearly and effectively.
15. Shares complete and up to date business information with all levels of the organization.
16. Focuses the organization on efforts that add value to the customer.
17. Accurately assesses customer needs through formal and informal means.
18. Consistently meets needs of internal customers.
19. Consistently thinks through meets the needs of external customers.
20. Thinks through issues without losing focus.
21. Makes decisions in a timely manner.
22. Provides accurate budgets for upcoming periods.
23. Manages resources to remain within budget goals.
24. Shows consistency between words and behaviors.
25. Follows through on commitments.
26. Acts on feedback from others.
27. Promotes an environment that supports a balance between work and personal life.

28. Rewards achievement based on performance and competence.
29. Celebrates significant organizational achievements.
30. Recognizes team accomplishments.
31. Monitors progress of others and redirects efforts when appropriate.
32. Provides clear feedback when performance standards are met.
33. Provides constructive feedback when performance standards are not met.
34. Ensures employees receive orientation and training necessary to be effective in their jobs.
35. Delegates responsibilities based on the skill level of direct reports.
36. Provides assistance and support to direct reports to carry out responsibilities.
37. Conducts formal performance reviews annually.
38. Sets high standards of performance for self.
39. Persists in achieving goals when faced with obstacles.
40. Provides others necessary support and authority to carry out their responsibilities.
41. Reduces obstacles that hinder performance of others.
42. Sets high performance standards for direct reports.
43. Establishes clear goals for work unit.
44. Uses a variety of tools including statistical methods to measure program results.
45. Translates strategic perspectives into pragmatic action plans.
46. Recruits and hires highly qualified people.
47. Recruits and maintains a diverse work force.
48 Fosters team work among direct reports.
49. Conducts meetings effectively.
50. Involves others in planning and problem solving.


The items where the FL group rated themselves significantly higher than the EL group.
1. Displays a thorough understanding of the industry's current environment.
2. Maintains a big picture view of the business.
3. Understands the financial implications of decisions.

4. Recognizes opportunities for global expansion and strategic alliances.
5. Anticipates problems and develops contingency plans.
6. Demonstrates a willingness to express unpopular points of view.
7. Acquires new funding for programs.

4. The fourth hypothesis was confirmed in the majority of cases. 15 of the 18 competencies targeted for growth showed significant growth over the 18 month period. Three competencies targeted for growth did not improve or were lowered in this period. See Figure B.

FIGURE B HERE

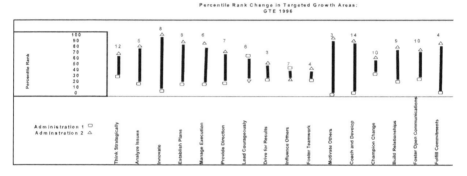

Percentile Rank Change in Targeted Growth Areas: GTE 1996

5. The fifth hypothesis was confirmed. The FL average self-ratings were 3.99. The colleague's average rating of the FL group was 3.53. This is significant at the p< .05 level.

Other findings not included in hypotheses
1. The clearest cut off of leadership groups was EL leaders: those in the top 20% as rated by Colleagues. This is different than the 10% division used in this study. The most accurate dividing point for the FL was supported as being the bottom 10%.
2. Average Leaders (AL) were those in the middle 70th percentiles.
3. A number of subjects retook the Multi Rater instrument on repeated occasions with an 18 month interval. Improvement within the same category range (EL, AL and FL) showed little overall improvement in the way they were viewed as leaders.

Those moving from one category (EL, FL and AL) to another on a business practice had a much greater impact on their constituent group.

4. The three competencies performed best by the EL group were Inspires Confidence, Builds Relationships and Drives for Results. This is consistent with the findings by Dirks (2000; 2002) who found that trust in leadership positively impacts team performance.

5. The three competencies performed worst by the FL group were Communicates the Vision; Empowers and Fosters Teamwork.

6. The one business practice that reached by far the highest level of significance in differentiating the two groups was, "Prepares people to understand the reason for change." This item was almost twice as important as the next most significant differentiator.

7. On test-retest the improvements that were significantly more noted and higher rated by colleagues were those that crossed a cusp from one zone (bottom 10%; middle 70%; highest 20%) to the higher one.

## Discussion

➤ Two statistically significantly different groups were identified as rated by their colleagues. The ELs did score themselves higher overall. However, there were 7 items where the FLs rated themselves significantly higher than the ELs as noted above. The items where the ELs rated themselves higher than the FLs seem to focus mainly on relationships, giving feedback, presenting a clear and effective vision. The items where the FLs rate themselves higher than the ELs focus on understanding the business, strategic insight and financial acumen. It should be noted that most all of the ELs higher self-rated business practices need to be done "out of the office" and involve interaction with co-workers.

➤ The competency that the ELs did best was Inspires Confidence. This is consistent with previous findings ( D.P. Campbell, 1991; Harris and Hogan, 1992; and Lombardo, Ruderman, and

McCauley, 1988) which indicate that a leader's trustworthiness and credibility is the single most important factor in the subordinates rating of his or her effectiveness. This is contrary to the Manager's rating which is most affected by technical competence (Harris and Schaubroeck, 1988).

➢ The FL group rated themselves higher than the EL group on several business practices. This despite the fact that all colleagues rated them much lower on these same practices. It would seem that this group deems these practices critical to business success and thus unrealistically prides themselves on their performance in these areas. This points to a significant philosophical difference in the FL group's idea of what makes a successful leader. The main difference is that FL led by analysis and independent work such as Balance Sheet review while ELs are out interacting with the work group. Therefore, a significant part of the FLs low scores may be due to the fact that they have incorrectly identified and are pursuing the wrong leadership practices.

➢ The significantly different self answer items between the EL and FL groups have been used to produce an instrument entitled The Leadership Success Inventory (LSI). Early small scale pilot studies with the LSI have been very effective in accurately identifying strong and weak leaders. An added validity aspect of the LSI is that all items were originally Multi-rater items and therefore judged to be critical business/leadership success factors. Thus the respondent cannot "fake good" in answering the items.

Key LSI Correlations Table

## Key LSI Correlations

| Key LSI Correlations | Q 11–14: Drives for results (Average non-self) | Q 28–30: Communicates vision (Average non-self) | Q 42–44: Empowers (Average non-self) | Q 45–48: Inspires confidence (Average non-self) | Q 49–54: Builds relationships (Average non-self) | Q 55–59: Fosters Teamwork (Average non-self) |
|---|---|---|---|---|---|---|
| Q 11–14: Drives for results (Average non-self) | — | | | | | |
| Q 28–30: Communicates vision (Average non-self) | 0.6544 | — | | | | |
| Q 42–44: Empowers (Average non-self) | 0.5225 | 0.7302 | — | | | |
| Q 45–48: Inspires confidence (Average non-self) | 0.6577 | 0.5957 | 0.6188 | — | | |
| Q 49–54: Builds relationships (Average non-self) | 0.6007 | 0.6707 | 0.65 | 0.8135 | — | |
| Q 55–59: Fosters Teamwork (Average non-self) | 0.4622 | 0.7833 | 0.7669 | 0.5805 | 0.6966 | — |

# COMPETENCIES INCLUDED IN THE STUDY & THEIR DEFINITIONS:

- ➤ **Aligns Strategy and Planning**. Translates strategic perspectives into pragmatic action plans. Allocates resources to tasks according to strategic priorities.
- ➤ **Analyzes Issues.** Understands complex concepts and relationships. Displays logical and analytical approaches to complex problems. Actively evaluates pros and cons of different options. Thinks through issues without losing focus. Understands the financial implications of decisions.
- ➤ **Attracts and develops talent.** Selects high caliber people. Provides challenging developmental opportunities for people. Provides clear feedback when performance standards are met. Provides constructive feedback when performance standards are not met.
- ➤ **Builds Relationships.** Treats others fairly and with respect. Is approachable. Develops effective working relationships with higher management. Develops effective working relationships with direct reports and other team members. Actively represents company in external relationships with agencies, government and community.
- ➤ **Champions continuous improvement.** Champions positive changes within the organization. Develops structures and processes to support change. Prepares people to understand the reason for change. Focuses the organization on efforts that add value to the customer.
- ➤ **Communicates Effectively.** Presents ideas clearly and effectively. Adjusts presentation of ideas to meet audience needs.
- ➤ **Communicates the Vision.** Conveys a sense of mission that inspires and motivates others. Communicates clearly about the future direction of the organization. Shares complete and up to date business information with all levels of the organization.
- ➤ **Demonstrates Adaptability and Flexibility**. Anticipates problems and develops contingency plans. Monitors progress of others and redirects efforts when appropriate. Recognizes when it is time to shift strategic direction.

- ➢ **Demonstrates Self Development.** Acts on feedback from others. Understands and compensates for own limitations. Demonstrates appropriate level of patience. Accepts criticism openly and non-defensively.

- ➢ **Drives for Results**. Sets high standards of performance for self. Works effectively under stress. Persists in achieving goals when faced with obstacles. Acts decisively.

- ➢ **Empowers.** Assigns responsibilities based on accurate assessment of the skill level of individuals. Provides others necessary support and authority to carry out their responsibilities. Removes obstacles that hinder the performance of others.

- ➢ **Fosters Teamwork.** Clearly defines roles and expectations of direct reports and other team members. Involves team in developing plans and making decisions. Recognizes team accomplishments. Promotes teamwork within the team. Builds collaborative relationships outside of functional area. Actively incorporates the perspective of others.

- ➢ **Innovates.** Creates innovative and creative solutions to problems. Recognizes opportunities for expansion and strategic alliances.

- ➢ **Inspires Confidence.** Demonstrates principled leadership and ethical behavior. Inspires the confidence and trust of others. Takes responsibility for own actions. Demonstrates consistency between words and behavior.

- ➢ **Leads Courageously**. Demonstrates willingness to express unpopular points of view. Supports risk taking by others. Takes business risks. Encourages others to make tough decisions.

- ➢ **Motivates.** Sets high standards of performance for others. Rewards achievement based on performance and competence. Creates an environment in which people perform beyond their own expectations. Celebrates significant organizational achievements.

- ➢ **Negotiates and Influences.** Encourages the open expression of ideas. Comprehends events, issues and opportunities from the viewpoint of others. Manages conflict situations effectively. Uses a variety of methods (e.g., persuasive arguments, modeling behavior and forming alliances) to gain support for ideas, strategies and values.

➢ **Thinks Strategically.** Stays abreast of global trends. Displays a thorough understanding of the industry's current environment. Maintains a big picture view of the business.

➢ **Values Diversity**. Assembles teams whose members have diverse and complimentary talents. Demonstrates respect and appreciation with differing backgrounds and experience. Creates an environment that supports a balance between work and home life.

# BIBLIOGRAPHY

Atwater, L.., Kenny, D. A., Malloy, T. E. (1988). Consensus in personality judgments at zero acquaintance. Journal of Personality and Social Psychology, 55, 378-395.

Bass, B. M. (1990) Bass and Sturgill's handbook of leadership (3rd edition). New York: Free Press.

Campbell, D. P., (1991) Manual of the Campbell Leadership Index. Minneapolis, Minnesota: National Computer Systems.

Chidester, T. R., Helmreich, R. L., Gregorich, S. E., & Geis, C. E. (1991). Pilot personality and crew coordination. International Journal of Aviation Psychology. 1, 25-44.

Colbert, Amy E., Witt, L.A., (2009). The Role of Goal Focused Leadership in Enabling the Expression of Conscientiousness. Journal of Applied Psychology, 94, 790-805.

Cooper, G. E., White, M. D., & Lauber, J. K. (Editors). (1979). Resource management on the flight deck (NASA Conference Publication #2120; NTIS # N80-22083). Moffett Field, CA: NASA-Ames Research Center.

DeVries, D. L. (1992). Executive selection: Advances but no progress. Issues and Observations, 12, 1-5.

Edwards, Jeffry R., Cable, Daniel M., (2009). The Value of Value Congruence. Journal of Applied Psychology, 94, 654-677.

Edwards, Jeffry R., Cable, Daniel M., (2009). The Value of Value Congruence. Journal of Applied Psychology, 94, 654-677.

Farh, J.L., & Dobbins, G.H. (1989). Effects of self-esteem on leniency bias in self-reports of performance: A structural equation model. Personnel Psychology, 42, 835-850.

Foushee, H.C., & Helmreich, R. L. (1988). Group interaction and flight crew performance. In E. L. Weiner & D. C. Nagel (Eds), Human factors in aviation (pp. 189-227). San Diego, CA: Academic Press.

Harris, G., & Hogan, J. (1992, April). Perceptions and personality correlates of managerial effectiveness. Paper presented at the 13th Annual Psychology in the Department Of Defense Symposium, Colorado Springs, CO.

Harris, M. M. & Schaubroeck, J. (1988). A meta analysis of self-supervisor, self-peer, and peer-supervisor ratings. Personnel Psychology, 41, 43-62.

Heidemeier, Heike, Moser, Klaus. (2009). Self-Other Agreement in Job Performance Ratings: A Meta-Analytic Test of a Process Model. Journal of Applied Psychology, 94, 353-370.

Howard, A. & Bray, D. W. (1990). Predictions of managerial success over long periods of time: Lessons from the management progress study. In K. E. Clark & M. B. Clark (Eds.), Measures of Leadership (pp. 113-130). West Orange, NJ: Leadership Library of America.

Hughes, R. L., Ginnett, R. A. & Curphy, G. J. (1993). Leadership: Enhancing the lessons of experience. Homewood, IL. Irwin.

Hurtz, Gregory M., Williams, Kevin J., (2009). Attitudinal and Motivational Antecedents of Participation in Voluntary Employee Development Activities. Journal of Applied Psychology, 94, 635-653.

Judge, T.A.; Bono, J.E.; Iles, R.; Gerhardt, M.W. (2002). Personality and Leadership: A Qualitative Review. Journal of Applied Psychology.

Liao, Hui, Toya, Keiko, Lepak, David P., Hong, Ying. (2009). Do They See Eye to Eye? Management and Employee Perspectives of High-Performance Work Systems and Influence Process on Service Quality. Journal of Applied Psychology, 94, 371-391.

Lombardo, M. M., Ruderman, M. N., & McCauley, C. D. (1998). Explanations of success and derailment in upper level management positions. Journal of Business and Psychology, 2, 199-216.

Nilsen, D. & Campbell, D. P. (1993). Self-observer rating discrepancies: Once an overrater always an overrater? Human Resource Management, 32, 265-281.

Peterson, D. B. (1993). Measuring change: A psychometric approach to evaluating individual training outcomes. In V. Arnold (Chair), Innovations in training evaluation: New measures, new designs. Symposium conducted at the Eighth Annual Conference of the Society for Industrial and Organizational Psychology. San Francisco.

Peterson, D.B., & Hicks, M. D. (May, 1993). Hoe to get people to change. Workshop presented at the Eighth Annual Conference of the Society for Industrial and Organizational Psychology. San Francisco.

Scott, Brent A., Colquitt, Jason A., Paddock, E. Layne, (2009). An Actor-Focused Model of Justice Rule Adherence and Violation: The Role of Managerial Motives and Discretion. Journal of Applied Psychology, 94, 756-769.

Shipper, F. & Wilson, C. L. (1991, July). The impact of managerial behaviors on group performance, stress and commitment. Paper presented at the Impact of Leadership Conference Center for Creative Leadership Conference, Center for Creative Leadership, Colorado Springs, Colorado.

Silverthorpe, (2001). Situational Leadership Style as a Predictor of Success Among Taiwanese Business Organizations. Journal of Psychology, 135, 399-413.

Sorcher, M. (1985). Predicting executive success: what it takes to make it in senior management. New York: Wiley.

Van Velsor, E., Taylor, S., & Leslie, J. B. (1992, August). Self-rater agreement, self awareness and leadership effectiveness. Paper presented at the 100th Annual Convention of the American Psychological Association, Washington, D. C.

Yukl, G. A. (1989). Leadership in Organizations (2nd edition). Englewood Cliffs, NJ: Prentice Hall.

# INDEX

**David Sullivan, PhD**

Dave was most recently the Executive Vice President of Executive and Leadership Development at one of the United States' largest Financial Services organizations, which he joined in 2005. During his tenure Dave has led the development and execution of the Executive Development strategy ranked in the top 10 nationally by *Leadership Excellence.*

In his unusually wide-ranging career Dave has served as business consultant, corporate president, clinical psychologist and graduate school professor. He previously served as President of Redirections, Inc. for 11 years. Redirections is a boutique consulting firm in Chicago specializing in Executive Coaching, Succession Planning, Strategic Planning, 360 Feedback and Leadership Development.

Dave has provided direct services to many major companies such as Motorola and Verizon in over 25 countries. He has significant experience working with C-level; executives to rethink strategy and lead change, and is in demand as a speaker. This combination of experiences makes Dave the perfect Mr. Inside/Mr. Outside.

Dave is an avid handball player who has recently moved to Las Vegas where he hopes to find more suitable competition than he did in Los Angeles.

**Don Double, M.A.**

Don Double, M.A. serves as President of Redirections, Inc. For over 23 years, Don has worked with managers and executives from Fortune 500 companies and government organizations helping them develop their leadership skills. He has coached over 5,000 senior and midlevel executives on leadership issues.

Prior to joining Redirections, Don worked as a member of the Hay Group in Chicago. Later, he founded Career Transition Consultants, which for seven years provided career related services for executives. He merged his business with Redirections, Inc. in 1988.

Don's work has included developing state of the art Executive and Managerial Development programs. He has experience in designing and delivering performance management systems, executive development systems, high-potential development and customized 360 Feedback programs.

He is the co-author of the Leadership Success Indicator, a scientifically validated instrument that predicts the likely success of an individual as a leader in a management or executive role.

Don has a Masters Degree in Counseling. Don has authored two books on managing careers published by the American Medical Association for medical practitioners seeking career change.

Don lives in Westmont, Illinois with his wife of 20 years.

### Jonathan Magid

Jonathan holds a Master's Degree in Organization Development from the Fielding Graduate University in Santa Barbara, CA. He lives and works in the Dallas, Texas area where he has recently been responsible for creating and executing the Associate Engagement strategy for one of the country's largest financial services firms. In prior roles Jonathan has designed and delivered leadership development programs ranked in the top-ten nationally for large institutions by *Leadership Excellence* magazine. He has successfully designed and led numerous organization and communication interventions yielding increased performance, employee, and customer satisfaction.

Jonathan has been a passionate advocate for exemplary leadership throughout the course of his career, which spans creative, operational, consulting, and management roles in industries ranging from film and television to technology and banking.

He can easily be persuaded to stop what he is doing and go fly fishing.

# ACKNOWLEDGMENTS

Dave thanks wife Beth and sons Dave Jr. and Brian for their support, patience and input during a year's long process. Dave Jr. supplied the bulk of the statistical analysis used in the study. Beth and Brian spent a good deal of time creatively brainstorming book titles (none of which were used but it was fun). My partner Don was a major part of the coaching, data collection and development of the LSI instrument. Jonathan brought a true writers touch to Dave's bone dry scientific prose. Thanks to all.

Don thanks Chrys for her constant support over the years even when the research and writing of this book seemed to test all of the authors. I also want to thank the Redirections team whose data collection and coaching made this possible and for Dave's research expertise, and Dave Jr, his son, who lent his excellent skills in data formatting and analysis that helped us "see" the insights described in this book.

Jonathan thanks Don and Dave for their patience, their feedback, and of course, the research that made this book possible. More than anyone else, Jonathan thanks Linda for being the steady, powerful light ashore, and for always shining brightest when he is farthest out to sea.

# FOR MORE INFORMATION

Contact Don Double
Redirections Inc.
663 Citadel Dr.
Westmont, IL  60559
donldouble@redirectionsinc.com
630-310-8481